Edwin James Stanley

Rambles in wonderland

A trip through the great Yellowstone National Park

Edwin James Stanley

Rambles in wonderland
A trip through the great Yellowstone National Park

ISBN/EAN: 9783337197605

Printed in Europe, USA, Canada, Australia, Japan

Cover: Foto ©Andreas Hilbeck / pixelio.de

More available books at **www.hansebooks.com**

EDWIN J. STANLEY.

OR, A TRIP THROUGH

The Great Yellowstone National Park.

WITH DESCRIPTIONS OF THE

Geysers, Mammoth Hot Springs, Boiling Caldrons, Lakes, Cataracts, Cañons, and Other Curiosities of this Remarkable Region;

CONTAINING

SKETCHES OF THE CROW INDIANS, THE GREAT YELLOWSTONE VALLEY, THRILLING ADVENTURES, INCIDENTS, AND ANECDOTES OF LIFE IN THE MOUNTAINS;

WITH AN

ACCOUNT OF THE CAPTURE AND SUFFERINGS OF A PARTY OF TOURISTS BY THE NEZ-PERCE INDIANS, UNDER CHIEF JOSEPH, IN 1877.

ALSO,

DIRECTIONS FOR TOURISTS

CONCERNING ROUTES, DISTANCES, OUTFITS, EXPENSES, AND OTHER USEFUL INFORMATION ABOUT THE PARK.

BY

EDWIN J. STANLEY.

MAP AND TWELVE ILLUSTRATIONS. FIFTH EDITION.

NASHVILLE, TENN.:
PUBLISHING HOUSE OF THE METHODIST EPISCOPAL CHURCH, SOUTH.
BARBEE & SMITH, AGENTS.
1898.

COPYRIGHT BY
E. J. STANLEY,
1878.

UPB

PREFACE.

On my return from a trip to the Yellowstone and through the National Park, I concluded to write up a few brief sketches of the more interesting features of that remarkable region, and the thrilling events of the journey, for the benefit of friends in the States. In spite of all efforts to condense, the "brief sketches" grew into a series of long letters, some of which appeared in a leading newspaper of the West. The general favor with which the letters were received, prompted a request for their publication in book-form. With some hesitancy the work of revision was commenced, and this volume is the result. It makes no claim to special literary merit, but is sent out with the firm belief that it will fill a place hitherto unoccupied, and with the hope that it will afford instruction and entertainment to the lovers of Nature everywhere, especially the youth of the land.

The author is pleased to acknowledge his indebtedness to the published reports of Dr. F. V. Hayden, United States

Geologist, for valuable data in the make-up of the work; also to Hon. N. P. Langford for some extracts from his glowing descriptions which appeared in *Scribner's Monthly*, and to other friends for substantial favors and encouragement in the enterprise.

E. J. S.

WHITEHALL, MONTANA TERRITORY, *July* 10, 1877.

CONTENTS.

CHAPTER I.

First Day. — Bozeman. — Gallatin. — Yellowstone. — Indians. — Camp on Shields River . . . . PAGE 7

CHAPTER II.

The Ranch.—Hot Springs.—Trout-Fishing.—Bozeman's Fate.—Thrilling Escape.—Yellowstone Valley.—Future Population 14

CHAPTER III.

The Crow Agency.—The Council.—The Treaty.—Novel Scenes.—Indian Character.—Names, Sagacity, and Eloquence.—Blackfoot 22

CHAPTER IV.

Indian Habits, Customs, and Beliefs.—Rescue of Two Captive Women.—Peace Policy.—Matrimony lively.—The Arrow *vs.* the Idea.—Missionaries.—Passing away 34

CHAPTER V.

Up the Yellowstone alone.—Meeting Indians.—Immigrant Gulch.—Wild Mountains.—Frontier Christians.—The Irrepressible Itinerant Preacher.—Cinnabar Mountain.—Devil's Slide 43

CHAPTER VI.

A Party of Tourists.—Mountain Transportation.—"Roughing it."—Personal Narrative.—Mammoth Hot Springs. — The Natural Wonder and Beauty of the West 52

CHAPTER VII.

The National Park.—Tower Falls.—Old Castles.—Bold Adventure.—Devil's Hoof.—Rare Jewels.—Petrifaction 62

CHAPTER VIII.

Mount Washburn.—Sublime Scenery.—Grand Cañon.—Upper Falls.—Perilous Position.—Great Falls . . . . PAGE 68

CHAPTER IX.

Dr. Hayden's Theory of the Falls and Cañon.—Lost again.—Camp on the Yellowstone.—Sulphur Mountain.—Mud-Volcano.—Giant's Caldron.—Muddy Geyser.—Diabolical Appearance of Everything 79

CHAPTER X.

Alum Creek.—Interesting Group of Hot Springs.—The "Flutter-Wheel."—Our Guide.—Mary's Lake.—Lower Geyser Basin.—Thud-Geyser.—The Fountain.—"Young Hopeful."—Journey up the River.—Vexations of the Way.—Tumble in the Mud.—Captain C——'s Misfortune.—Boiling Lakes.—Arrival at Upper Basin.—Wonderful Change 89

CHAPTER XI.

Upper Geyser Basin.—Meeting with Friends.—Our Camp "Doing" the Geysers.—"Old Faithful."—The Sentinel.—First Eruption witnessed.—Description.—The Crater.—Ornamentation of the Mound.—Beehive.—Giantess.—Fearful-looking Cavity.—Langford's Description.—Refusal to accommodate Less Distinguished Personages.—Castle Geyser.—Beautiful Mound-Spring 97

CHAPTER XII.

Curiosity.—New Mode of Washing.—Cooking in a Geyser.—Disappointed Expectations—Dish-Washing.—Bridget takes Revenge.—"Taken in."—Grand Geyser.—Turban.—The Saw-Mill, *alias* "Rustler."—Old Chimneys.—Extinct Geysers.—Amusing Incident.—"Attack in the Rear."—"Change of Base."—River-side.—Comet.—Fantail Geyser.—The Grotto.—Quaint Formation.—The Giant Geyser, the Grandest in the World.—Wonderful Eruption.—Two Hundred and Fifty Feet in the Air.—Intense Excitement 107

CHAPTER XIII.

Sunrise Eruptions.—Moonlight.—Firelight.—Sleeping among the Geysers.—A Californian.—The Name Geyser.—Geysers of Iceland.—Queries answered.—Breaking through.—Theory of Geyser-Eruption.—In Camp 118

CHAPTER XIV.

Homeward bound.—Our Caravan.—Novel Way of Traveling.—Variety the Spice of Life.—Cayuses.—"Bucking" Propensities.—Noble Animals.—Camp-Life: its Pleasures.—A Pleasant Party.—Dream fulfilled.—Narrow Escape of "the Judge" 124

CHAPTER XV.

Trip to the Yellowstone Lake.—Description of the Lake.—Dimensions.—Depth.—Huge Bear-Tracks.—A Cold Bath.—Swans and other Water-fowls.—Swarms of Trout.—Intestinal Affection.—Not hungry for Fish.—Numerous Islands.—Mr. Stevenson's Visit.—Wild Beasts.—Once trod by the Red-Man.—Tradition.—Hot Spring in the Lake.—Cooking Fish.—Mountaineer's Idea of the Lake.—Conjecture.—Mr. Everts's Adventure.—Is lost, and wanders for Thirty-seven Days.—Lives on Thistle-Roots.—Attacked by a Mountain-Lion.—Thrilling Account.—Miraculous Deliverance.—Splendid Place in which to spend the Summer.—Mountains.—Inspiring Scenes . . . . PAGE 133

CHAPTER XVI.

Lake-Shore.—Hunting.—The Bear.—The Moose.—Mountain-Grouse.—"Fool-Hens."—Sage-Chickens.—Panther or Mountain-Lion.—Lassoing a Bear.—Beaver.—Their Homes.—Industry.—Desolation.—Charming Solitude.—Homeward bound.—Camping in the Rain.—Return to Mammoth Springs.—The Parting.—On to Bottler's Ranch.—Preaching on Sunday.—A Refreshing Time.—Indian "Scare."—A Stampede.—Running for Life.—Arrival at Bozeman.—Cordial Reunions.—Ample Compensation 142

CHAPTER XVII.

Hitherto Obscurity of the Geyser Region.—The Cause.—Legends.—Magic Cities.—Mysterious Inhabitants.—Jim Bridger.—Other Mountaineers visit this Region.—First Expedition.—Second.—Dr. Hayden's Expedition.—The National Park.—Its Variety of Wonders.—The Grandest in the World.—Grand Exposition 151

CHAPTER XVIII.

THRILLING ADVENTURES OF EXCURSIONISTS IN THE NATIONAL PARK.—Nez-Percé Indians under Joseph.—Capture of Radersburg Party.—Bloody Work.—Mrs. Cowan, her Sister, and Brother, in Captivity.—Release of Captives.—Cowan's Miraculous Escape.—Radersburg Party attacked.—Kenck killed.—Escape of the Others.—Hardships endured.—Deitrich's Death.—Shiveley's Account of his Captivity 157

LIST OF ILLUSTRATIONS.

	PAGE
Map of Yellowstone Park................................*Face Title-page.*	
The Yellowstone..... .... *Face*	19
White Mountain, Mammoth Springs............................	52
Tower Falls..	64
Cliffs of the Yellowstone.......................................	68
Upper Falls, Yellowstone.......................................	72
Lower Falls, Yellowstone.......................................	73
Great Cañon of the Yellowstone...............................	79
The "Giantess"..	102
Mud-Springs	105
In the Geyser Basin......	111
The "Giant" Geyser	113
Yellowstone Lake..	133

CHAPTER I.

First Day.—Bozeman.—Gallatin.—Yellowstone.—Indians.—Camp on Shields River.

"NATURE never repeats herself, you know."

"Do you mean that nowhere in the wide world can be found two things just alike?"

"Exactly. Nature defies all theories, and theories balk and blunder in the presence of the endless forms and varieties of life in which she scorns duplicates."

"Surely, doctor, you do not intend to bewilder me with your philosophy upon the threshold of our rambles, and before we have completed our outfit?"

"No, no, my young friend, but I desire to prepare you for a proper appreciation of the unequaled wonders of the region through which you are to ramble, and which has not inaptly been termed 'Wonderland.' Those who have visited Colorado, California, Utah, and the famed resorts in the East and in Europe, can form but little conception of the wonders that abound throughout these Western wilds. In no country on the globe, within the same area, has Nature crowded so much of grandeur and majesty, with so much of novelty and variety. Unlike any other scenery of the world, and unrivaled in wild and weird wonders, the Upper Yellowstone, the geysers, the mountains, lakes, and valleys, of this country will always draw the lovers of the marvelous in Nature—"

"But stop, doctor; here are Pat and the boys all ready for the start, and I fear your enthusiasm will exhaust itself before we reach this wonderland." By this time Dr. H——'s two little sons and his man Pat reined up in our presence with a two-horse wagon and a saddled horse behind, ready to convey us down the Yellowstone, forty-five miles, to the doctor's ranch.

We had spent several days in Bozeman, a prosperous and pretty little town of one thousand inhabitants, named in honor of a young man from the South whose name was Bozeman. He was a fearless adventurer, and led the first expedition of gold-hunters to the Gallatin Valley, by the Powder River, Big Horn, and Yellowstone route, which afterward bore the name of the "Bozeman Road." The town is located on a beautiful plateau, between the East and West Forks of the Gallatin River, and not far from a lofty range of snow-crowned mountains lying to the southward. Bozeman has grown to be the business metropolis of Eastern Montana, supplying the Yellowstone and Gallatin Valleys, and the military fort three miles away on the East Fork of the Gallatin.

Tuesday morning, August 11, 1873, we left Bozeman and crossed the foot-hills to Fort Ellis. This is one of the principal military posts of the Western frontier. It commands the whole country embraced in the Upper Yellowstone Valley, and the three forks of the Missouri, including some of the finest and most productive country in the Territory. There were three or four hundred soldiers at the fort when we passed. It was just haying-time, and as I saw the loaded wagons rolling into the stack-yard, and several wrecks by the road-side, how vividly I was reminded of the mishaps, upsettings, and adventures of my youthful days when I hauled hay to Fort Leavenworth!

Dr. H—— reminded me that expeditions against the Indians and for exploration purposes were outfitted here, and that troops were often sent to escort expeditions up the Yellowstone and into the " regions beyond."

" Faith, and hadn't ye betther be afther hevin' an ethscort for the likes o' us?" queried Pat, as he contemplated the possibility of losing his sandy scalp somewhere in that wilderness, which in his imagination was always peopled with savage redskins.

" Don't you think, Pat, we are sufficiently protected by our Enfield rifles?" asked the doctor, rather carelessly.

" Sure, thin, I am; the rafle must indade have a mon at the tother eend, and thin, sometimes, oftin the scalp goes off before the gun."

" But, Pat, the red-skin would not want a Paddy's scalp to ornament his belt."

" And by the blissid Vargin it's a bit betther than yer own, docther, with yer bawld head."

By this time we had passed the busy, bustling fort with its stacks of steel and hay, the boys had settled back into their seats, and we had struck the Bozeman Pass. High mountains on either side shut out from view the fort, the valley, and the extended landscape, and we were confined to a somewhat narrow defile, with a clear, cool trout-stream singing its rippling way beside and often across our road, fed by the perpetual snow that crowned the mountain thousands of feet above us. Now and then we emerged from the deep gorge, and reached a higher knoll, from which the prospect enlarged to loveliness and sometimes grew into grandeur. Upon turning our eyes, the famed Gallatin Valley burst upon our vision, perhaps the richest and most beautiful in the Territory. It varies from ten to twenty-five miles in width, and is nearly forty miles in length, extending from southeast to northwest. It is noted for the productiveness of its soil and the beauty of its scenery. The vast area of plain, including the gentle, swelling foot-hills, was flecked with herds of cattle, farm-houses, ranch-cottages, and vast fields waving with golden grain ripe unto the harvest. Enterprise and thrift had made this wilderness to bloom and the desert to rejoice and blossom as the rose. Advancing civilization has already planted here and there the nuclei of "future great" cities, and relieves the dull and monotonous outline of swelling foot-hills, making bright contrasts in the distant landscape. The valley is inclosed by lofty and rugged mountain-ranges, rising on the east and south like huge walls of defense. The Madison, Jefferson, Bowlder, and Crow Creek Ranges, not only lift their snow-capped peaks high into the western sky, but the two former give a Western immortality to the names of two of the honored Presidents of the land of the early free. The mountain scenery from this valley surpasses anything we have yet seen—the ranges rising peak above peak as they recede in the distance, and standing azure-hued and snow-crowned in their grandeur, some of them a hundred miles away. Bozeman and his comrades must have been filled with enthusiasm when, so near the close of a long and perilous journey, through the wilderness inhabited by hostile savages, this lovely valley, spread out in all its natural beauty, burst upon their vision. It was then but a wilderness, and they deserve immortality for opening it to productive civilization.

The expedition sent across the continent by Mr. Astor, in 1811, under Captain Wilson P. Hunt, did not discover this valley, nor that of Captain Bonneville in 1833. Captain Reynolds, who commanded the expedition sent out by the Government in 1860, to explore the Yellowstone, crossed this valley from the head of Wind River on his way to the three forks of the Missouri, and thence to the head-waters of the Yellowstone.

"What a splendid country for railroads!" exclaimed the doctor, as we crossed the divide through a low gap that formed a natural road-bed with easy grades out of the valley. "Railroads can be built here with as little cost as in what are called level countries, and the resources developed in this country would rival the wealth of Indus."

"Did you ever read 'The First Families of the Sierras?'" I asked, looking the doctor in the face quizzically.

"No: what of them?"

"Nothing, only one character struck me with much force as peculiarly Western. He was called 'Judge,' and attributed everything to the 'glorious climate of Californy,' and thought nothing impossible to 'this glorious climate of Californy!'"

"But," interrupted the doctor, "I do not mean the 'climate of Montana,' yet I am satisfied with it as the equal of California, or Italy, as to that."

"You see the point, then—" The boys had discovered a little streamlet of sparkling water with grassy banks, and were eager to stop for lunch. Pat grazed the ponies, and after an hour's rest we moved on down the stream, and, passing one or two cabins, the doctor pointed out the lone grave of a colonel in the United States Army who in a fight with hostile Indians several years ago was decoyed from his retreat by the treacherous savages and shot. A few miles on, the bluffs on either side of us began to widen, and we soon emerged into the famous valley of the Yellowstone. We reached the river a short distance below the point where it rushes through a rugged cañon, and takes its leave of the principal range of the Rocky Mountains.

As I approached the far-famed Yellowstone my emotions were indescribable. In my boyhood I had read of the wonderful adventures for which it had become historic, and had cherished a consuming desire to visit this far-away Western river, walled in by rugged mountains, and fed by perpetual snows; whose banks had for generations been trodden only by savage Sioux, Crows, and Blackfeet, and had echoed only to their fierce war-whoop, and to which the bravest "pale-face" scarcely dared adventure himself until only a few years ago. I stood on its banks in silence, with the strange sensation of boyish ambition realized thrilling my soul, until the doctor called my attention to the fact that the waters that rushed so rapidly over the rocky bottom at our feet came from the Wind River Mountains and flowed into the Missouri, the Mississippi, and on to the Gulf of Mexico, traveling a distance of nearly four thousand miles.

The river here is one hundred and fifty yards wide and bordered by cottonwood. On the opposite side is the reservation of the Crow nation, long one of the most powerful and savage of all the Indian tribes of the West. The United States commissioners were now at their agency, twelve miles down the river, negotiating a treaty for their lands south of the Yellowstone; while the larger portion of the tribe had just returned from their hunting-grounds and lined the opposite bank of the river for miles with their lodges, or *tepees*, with the valley and foot-hills beyond darkened with herds of ponies.

The cabin of the hunter and ranchman and the tent of bold prospecters stood hard by the few straggling lodges on this side. As we passed down toward the agency we met bands of Indians roaming all through the country, and I could not help thinking what a picture of the "irrepressible conflict" between advancing civilization and sullen savagery was now before me! The white man crowding the Indian back toward the setting sun, reclaiming his wilderness to useful tillage, exterminating his game, subduing his forests, converting his rivers into commercial arteries, his valleys into fields of golden grain, mining his mountains, and extending the arts of civilized industry all over the country—

the whole picture was here epitomized along the banks of the wildest of all the rivers of the continent. The soft sentimentalism which romance has thrown over the untutored tribes of the forest melts away like morning mists before the demands of a brighter and better civilization, and we pity the victims of savage life who must be destroyed because they will not be subdued and civilized.

At nightfall we camped on Shields River, a bold, rapid mountain-stream, which heads in a snowy range away to the northwest. The first night out in camp in a country filled with savage men and beasts is not the most favorable for sound, refreshing sleep. Around the glaring camp-fire, with thousands of restless Crows not many miles away, and savage beasts, possibly, nearer, we could not indulge much in the traditional yarns of camp-life. The horses were hobbled out, the boys tucked away in their "little bed;" the doctor and I rolled ourselves up in the only buffalo-robe and went to sleep, "sweetly dreaming," while Pat sat silently and wakefully upon his dignity, apparently impressed with his great responsibility as much as was he who guarded Francis I. on the fatal night of Pavia—

". . . . who his sleepless vigils kept,
While lords and ladies wailed and wept."

CHAPTER II.

The Ranch.—Hot Springs.—Trout-Fishing.—Bozeman's Fate.—Thrilling Escape.—Yellowstone Valley.—Future Population.

THE next morning, refreshed, but breakfastless, a drive of ten miles down the river and across the foot-hills of Sheep Mountain, with Crazy Mountain twelve miles away to the north, brought us to the doctor's ranch, where we did ample justice to a sumptuous repast, relished keenly after the long fast.

The doctor's ranch is on a small stream three miles north of the Yellowstone, at a point where two large veins of hot sulphur-water boil up from the earth. These springs possess valuable medicinal properties, and induced the doctor to venture so far beyond the bounds of civilization and expose himself and family to the privations and perils of frontier-life in the very presence of hostile Indians. Surprised to see such extensive improvements out here in this wilderness, twenty miles from the nearest house, save the Crow Agency, and forty miles from any other family, I asked an explanation.

"You see," said the doctor, "I came to Montana in '64, discovered these hot sulphur-springs, and, believing that the Northern Pacific Railroad would soon be constructed across this country, and that this extensive and fertile valley would be opened for settlement, I resolved to secure what I thought would some day be a valuable property."

"Niver a railroad," interposed Pat—"niver a railroad cum to these diggin's; but the painted savages they did cum, and a pickle they made of us, indade, the red-skins."

"Yes, it is true, the railroad never came, but the Indians did, and we had a narrow escape with our lives. They ran off my stock, and destroyed part of my improvements."

"But it was the scalps upon our heads, it was, the 'tarnal crathurs was afther; and, howly Vargin presarve us! we have our hair on yit, we have, sparin' the docther."

We found a week's enjoyment at the doctor's ranch, hunting and fishing. The streams abound with choice mountain-trout, which are finely flavored. They are of a light-gray color, changing into a bright yellow below, and beautifully speckled. They are quite game, average one pound and a half, and pull splendidly on a line. This species of trout abounds on the western slope, but is rare east of the mountains. Antelope and deer are plentiful, though it requires skill to take them. We were fortunate enough to bring in two splendid antelopes. Crazy Mountain, which appears to be a cluster of rugged mountains thrown together in wildest confusion, offers a fine retreat for the elk and bear, where they flourish in great numbers. We longed for a wild-bear hunt, with its adventures and perils; but neither time nor the weather favored the sport, and we had to be content with the many thrilling stories told us of the fortune and fate of the bold hunters who have been reckless enough to venture amid the rugged wilds of the Rocky Mountains.

About seventy miles below here the gallant Bozeman met his sad, sad fate. Passing down the valley one day to the old Bozeman crossing on the Yellowstone, the extinguished camp-fires, an old wagon-tire, and other *débris*, recalled the fate of the bold adventurer; and a friend, whose knowledge of the early pioneers and their fate is equaled only by the relish with which he tells the story of their exploits, gave the following story:

A warm friend of Bozeman, who lived in Gallatin Valley, desired to go down the Yellowstone to Fort Smith on business. It was a dangerous route, and nothing would do but Bozeman must go with him, as he was an experienced mountaineer and a good Indian fighter. At first he declined, saying that he would never return. He seemed to have a presentiment of his fate, though he at last yielded to the urgent entreaties of his friend. He remarked to his friends on starting that they would never see his face again.

The two proceeded down the river in safety about eighty miles, when one day, just after making a hearty lunch, they saw a party of Indians approaching, whom they at first supposed to be friendly. On discovering their mistake, Bozeman's companion fled and escaped, and he stood alone, powerless and speechless, making no resistance while they coolly disarmed him and then took his life. Thus perished one of the boldest and bravest of pioneers.

While here, another incident of thrilling interest is called up. It was related to me by E. G. Brooke, Esq., a well-known citizen of Montana, and is in substance as follows:

In the spring of 1866 a party of twenty persons, including two women and five children, descended the Yellowstone in a "Mackinaw," returning to the States. About seventy miles below here, and near the place where poor Bozeman afterward fell, they were attacked by a large band of Sioux Indians. One of the men was killed outright, and the rest abandoned the boat with everything except what they could carry on their persons, and fled toward the settlements. With one sick man, two women, and five helpless children, harassed by the savages, facing a piercing March wind rendered doubly severe by a blinding snow-storm, living on raw elk-meat at half-rations, trudging through mud and snow, over rocks and cactus, half clad and half starved, for eight days and nights, clinging to life and yet expecting every day to be scalped, they excited the liveliest sympathy and the deepest interest. Strange to say, they came into such deep distress that some of the men seriously proposed to abandon the women and children to their fate, and make good their own escape. To this proposition a rough-looking, noble-hearted man replied: "My friends, I could never go home and tell my wife and children that I had been craven-hearted enough to leave two poor women and their children to perish in the wilderness. No, never! I will stand by them and perish with them if the worst comes to the worst." The cowards slunk away from his presence until they could catch the spirit of his heroism, and then returned one by one and pledged their lives for the protection of the defenseless. This lion-hearted man at once became their leader, carrying his food and gun with three hundred cartridges, his blankets and frying-pan by day, giving his blankets to the women and children at night, and keeping watch with his trusty gun over them while they caught the hasty, heavy sleep necessary to strengthen them for their perilous journey. They crossed the river near the spot where we now stand, the men wading through the cold, dashing, dangerous billows, bearing the helpless members of the party in their arms, and making several trips before the last one was safely over.

The same was repeated at Shields River, and scarcely had they reached the west bank of the latter stream with their charge when the savages came up to the east bank from which they had just escaped. After much privation and suffering they were rescued by a party who, with provisions and clothing, had been sent from Bozeman for their relief. Much of the time the women and children marked the frozen ground with their bare, bleeding feet.

One incident of this perilous journey through the wilderness is worth relating. One night around their camp-fire, when everything was still and solemn as death, a member of the party in a full, clear voice, struck up—

> "When marshaled on the nightly plain,
> The glittering hosts bestud the sky," etc.

One of the ladies joined in with a soft, tender voice, and the effect was magical. As the notes of that grand old hymn that had guided so many bewildered souls to the Star of Bethlehem floated out on the night air that had so often trembled with the hideous yell of the savage, stout hearts were melted, and the souls of hardy men kindled with a purer faith and a sublimer courage. Thenceforth they could do, and dare, and die. Surely, this is one of the most thrilling incidents of pioneer-life in Montana.

The valley, stretching for many miles along the Yellowstone, is fertile and beautiful beyond description. When safe for the abode of white men, a vast domain of rich lands, stretching from the cañon above the mouth of Shields River to the mouth of Powder River, and including the Big Horn, Clark's Fork, and numerous smaller tributaries, will be settled up, and will support a dense population. Only think of it! Across these virgin lands no surveyor's chain has been stretched, and into this virgin soil no squatter's stake has been driven. We can now have pick and choice. But, with visions of cottages and mansions, and waving grain-fields, and luxurious wealth, that will some day abound here, before my mind, I went on my way singing:

> "No foot of land do I possess,
> No cottage in this wilderness—
> A poor wayfaring man!"

THE YELLOWSTONE.

The climate is humid and mild compared with the region nearer the mountains. The soil will produce all the cereals in abundance, and all the esculent roots and vines. The bottom-lands are richly supplied with willow, alder, thistles, hops, mint, peas, currants, gooseberries, service-berries, various species of thorn, and other fruit-bearing shrubs. The cottonwood grows to great size, and the chokecherry-bush discards its mountain modesty, and aspires to the proportions of a tree. The Yellowstone above the mouth of the Powder River sweeps through the country in long and majestic stretches, with a current of at least four miles an hour. Its bosom is studded with islands by hundreds, some of which are three and four miles long, and covered with cottonwood-groves; many of them are so handsome that the tourist is reminded of the well-kept grounds of an old English country-mansion. Indications of the presence of coal in abundance are met with near the Powder River, while sandstone-bluffs crop out along the Yellowstone above Tongue River, and limestone exists plentifully above Pompey's Pillar. Thirty miles above the mouth of the Big Horn may be regarded as the head-waters of navigation. The landscape scenery for hundreds of miles along the Yellowstone is unsurpassed in beauty and picturesque grandeur, until the traveler reaches the mouth of the Powder River, at which he strikes the region of country known as the "Mauvaises Terres," or Bad Lands, which, like much of the country on the Upper Missouri, presents to the eye the appearance of burnt plains broken by large ravines, and interspersed with immense benches of baked clay. "Here," says a traveler, "a sudden change takes place, and we are ushered from the highest state of verdure to that of extreme desolation; and it is, without exception, the most horrible-looking country I ever saw." Two or three days' drive from this point, and we reach the vast chain of yellow sandstone bluffs hundreds of feet high, bleak and bare, through which the river forces its passage, and from which it takes its name.

No country in the world presents such striking contrasts and varied scenery. The diversified conditions of climate, and products, and resources, indicate unmistakably that this vast Territory is specially adapted to a diversified industry, which always implies a self-sustaining and prosperous people. The future is as full of promise as the past has been rich in adventure.

There is no portion of Montana, nor any part of the mountains, better watered than this valley. "The mountains," says a writer, "are jeweled all over with copious springs as clear and cold as crystal ice. These countless fountains, uniting their currents above, come down, rushing through cañons and splashing over ledges, and traverse the valley like ribbons of silver. The water is transparent as glass, and the countless brooks abound with the finest trout." All the streams are lined more or less with timber; the land is gently undulating, and not a foot but can be easily irrigated if necessary. As I rambled over the foot-hills, I could but think that this vast stretch of rich country, which during ages past has been the undisputed abode of the wild red-man; these streams, on the banks of which he was born, and by the side of which he was reared; these plains, over which he roamed at will with the wild beasts that he loved to chase—all must soon come under the influence of civilization, and yield to the sceptre of the irrepressible white man. The words of Whittier came involuntarily into my mind:

> "I hear the tread of pioneers,
> Of nations yet to be—
> The first low wash of waves where soon
> Shall roll a human sea."

Ere another decade, thought I, the iron horse will go puffing and snorting through these valleys, drawing behind him the thundering train laden with curious travelers and burdened with the treasures of mountain and valley and the commerce of nations; these water-courses shall be lined with mills and manufactories propelled by their power, these landscapes flecked with herds of cattle and dotted with homes of prosperous pioneers; while on every hand will come up the din and whir of business, the evidences of a great and prosperous commonwealth.

Two expeditions have descended the Yellowstone for more than a hundred miles, one of which was the party surveying the route of the Northern Pacific Railroad, under a strong military force in charge of Colonel Baker, which went down during the summer of 1872, but after a hard-fought battle with the Sioux Indians, and losing several men, were compelled to return; the other, a party of prospecters going to look for gold in the vicinity of Tongue River, in the spring of 1874, but after a hard fight with the Indians, who were determined to resist them, and the loss of one man, they also were compelled to return. It is thought that gold in rich quantities abounds in the mountains below; and daring, restless adventurers will not be satisfied until the country is prospected.

CHAPTER III.

The Crow Agency.—The Council.—The Treaty.—Novel Scenes.—Indian Character.
—Names, Sagacity, and Eloquence.—Blackfoot.

On Saturday morning, in company with my friend the doctor, I rode over to the Crow Agency, which is about ten miles to the southeast, across the Yellowstone River, which we had to ford. This proved to be critical business, as the stream was swollen from recent rains above, and was much deeper than we expected to find it, and very rapid, though we escaped with no injury save a good drenching, and were grateful indeed to get free from the mad waves of the surging, turbulent river with no worse misfortune. These mountain-streams, rushing down over beds of huge bowlders, in many places with a descent that sends the surging volumes onward at a wonderful rate, are often dangerous to the life and property of him who ventures to cross them when swollen.

The improvements at the agency are a few large storehouses and residences for officers and employés—about twenty-five in number—arranged in the form of a square, with one side open, and about twenty or more small houses for the use of the Indians who may desire to live in them. There is also a farm of several hundred acres in cultivation, producing grain and vegetables; also a grist-mill located on the little stream hard by, that comes down from the cluster of rugged peaks rising up to the south. The houses are built of sun-dried bricks, and commonly known as adobe, or "doby," houses. The Indians prefer their lodges, and the out-buildings are seldom used except by the white men who have married squaws.

The council, which had been in session for a week, between the United States commissioners, of which Major Brunot was principal, and the chiefs and head-men of the Crow nation, had just concluded, and the treaty was signed only a few moments before we arrived. This is one of the most important treaties for the Government that have been made with the Indians for many years. By it all the country south of the Yellowstone River belonging to the Crows, embracing an area extending to the forty-fifth degree of north latitude on the south, to the mouth of the Big Horn on the east, amounting to more than six millions of acres, abounding in rich mineral lands, pasture-grounds, and fertile valleys, including Big Horn, Clark's Fork, Rosebud, and others, has been added to the public domain.*

The Crows get a reservation about half as large, which embraces the Judith Basin, a country away north toward the Missouri, and receive the interest, annually, on one million dollars for their support as long as they exist as a tribe.

I had the pleasure of meeting and talking with the commissioners, and made the acquaintance of the newly-appointed agent, who is a Methodist preacher. Several of the Indian tribes in Montana, according to the present policy, are partially under the supervision of the Methodist Episcopal Church. The sudden and wonderful change in the pecuniary circumstances of Indian agents, often from comparative poverty to wealth and affluence, enabling them to build costly mansions, give splendid entertainments, and fare sumptuously every day, and all on simply a living salary of fifteen hundred dollars a year, has aroused the suspicions of the public; and an honest man taking

* This treaty was not ratified by Congress, and did not take effect.

the position, even if he resists the temptations before him, becomes the subject of unpleasant surmises, severe and trying criticism, as well as the avowed and intense opposition of the "Indian Ring," whose purpose is to make the most of the present policy toward the red-men.

The Crows were long one of the most powerful of the Western Indian tribes. They roamed the Plains from the summit of the Rocky Mountains on the west to the borders of the more powerful Sioux nation on the east, and from the Judith River on the north to the Platte on the south, though their place of rendezvous has generally been about the Yellowstone and Big Horn Rivers. They have always been the deadly enemies of the Blackfeet, with which tribe they are now at war. They are now at war also with their neighbors the Sioux, whom they greatly fear, also with the Cheyennes and Arapahoes. For a long time they were the enemies of the whites, and for many years were the terror of the trapper and prospecter; and no doubt many a "pale-face" has quailed before their savage war-whoop and fallen the victim of their bloody scalping-knife. Bonneville speaks of an encounter with them, and Irving describes them as a treacherous and warlike tribe, horse-stealers of the first order, and easily provoked to acts of violence and bloodshed. I think that Stevens was annoyed by them, and one party of traders were relieved, while in their country, of all their valuables and accoutrements, narrowly escaping with their lives.

But since the treaty with them at Laramie, in 1865, they have professed great friendship for the whites, though accused of raids and various depredations commonly charged to the Sioux. A raid was made into the Gallatin Valley in the fall of 1871, in which two white men were killed, and a large herd of horses stolen. Several raids have been made since, by which horses were stolen. These misdemeanors have generally been charged to the Cheyennes and Sioux, but may have been committed by the Crows.

The Crows are said to be quite fond of practical jokes. A party of them met a white man on the prairie, and took his fine horse, equipments, clothes—everything—and gave him in return a complete Indian outfit. The transformation from a finely-mounted and well-dressed cavalier to a full suit of savage dress—hunting-shirt, breech-clout, leggins, moccasins, hat, and filthy blanket, mounted on a bony pony in primitive style and in a pitiable plight—was complete. In this predicament they left him with his scalp on, to indulge in such reflections as the occasion suggested, while a noble red-skin, dressed in the full suit of a civilized gentleman, and mounted on a splendid charger, rode away with the yelling crowd.

By war and pestilence this once numerous tribe has been reduced to less than four thousand, divided into two parties known as the Mountain and the River Crows, so called from the country occupied by them respectively.

They live and roam in separate companies, but are on good terms, and receive their annuities together. Both parties were represented in the recent council, and both signed the treaty. They had just returned from the buffalo-country, and the larger portion of the tribe were camped in the vicinity, their *tepees* arranged in promiscuous groups or villages along the river-bank for miles. All the chiefs, head-men, and warriors, with large numbers of women and children, were present at the agency, making the largest body of Indians I had ever seen, and especially of those who have scarcely emerged from a state of barbarism. Most of them are yet quite "primitive" in their appearance, and show but slightly the "genial influences of civilization."

It is customary after a treaty to make them a present of

some kind, and, as the commissioners had nothing else, the agent gave them a good supply of ammunition, which was just being distributed. It was a motley group, and a scene of confusion and uproar to one not accustomed to such exhibitions. Bands of marshaled and painted warriors stood or sat in circles, and were receiving each his quota of cartridges from the respective captain or chief. Old men worn out in the service, and no longer able to stand in the ranks and go out with the valiant braves, looked on with intense interest; squaws dressed in every conceivable manner, and rolling in filth, many of them with papooses strapped on their backs, and looking more like slaves, wandered hither and thither in every direction; while scores of half-clad, happy little urchins were bounding nimbly about, shooting their arrows, indulging in their playful sports, shouting at the top of their voices, and having a good time generally. Horsemen moved to and fro, and everything for the time seemed to be full of excitement. First one, and then another, mounting a barrel, a goods-box, or a pony, would harangue the crowd. This speech-making they seemed to consider quite an honor, and enjoyed it hugely. Some of them were good orators, in their tongue, and by their flow of language commanded silence and respectful attention whenever they talked, and I longed to know what they said. Others had but little magnetism, and attracted no attention by their harangues. Some of them appeared to be greatly dissatisfied with the treaty, and the people feared that they would, in their excitement, be tempted to acts of violence.

I saw all of the chiefs, and was formally introduced by a friend to many of them. Some of them appeared quite cordial in their manner, and a number of them manifested a good degree of intelligence in their way. Of course, they are untutored and uncultivated, and are ignorant of the white man's ways; but those who think the Indian a fool in every respect are greatly mistaken.

There are a number of them called chiefs, and they seem to have degrees of rank among them similar to the officers of an army. In time of war they have one head-chief, and all the rest command squads under him, and are subject to his orders. Then they have what are called head-men, who I suppose are something like "high privates," and generally sit in councils and sign treaties. In time of peace the tribe is divided into parties, or bands, under the leadership of the various chiefs. They are not distinguished by their dress, though some of the chiefs have costly attire, all beaded, colored, feathered, and finished up in the highest style of Indian art, which, however, is only worn on special occasions. In time of battle they are often attired in the most gorgeous manner. Imagine him with a beaded robe, leggins, moccasins, belt, arrow-case, and his face painted, person ornamented with feathers and glittering trinkets—pieces of silver, tin, and shells—and all crowned with a flowing head-dress of eagle's-feathers arranged in genuine savage style, perhaps trailing the ground behind when he walks, together with shield, gun, and accoutrements, and ornaments, mounted on a fiery charger, decked out in corresponding style—and you have an idea of the royal appearance of an Indian dignitary, who feels as proud and as great as a king upon his throne. Such an outfit, too, is quite costly. In a battle down on the Yellowstone in 1872 a Sioux chief was killed, and a soldier was offered a hundred and fifty dollars for his head-dress alone.

Their names are after the Indian style, and some of them rather singular, though often suggestive. Some of them are: Blackfoot (Kam-ne-but'-se), Iron Bull (Che-ve-te-pu-ma'-ta), Long Horse (E-she-te-hat'-se), Show-his-face (In-te'-us), Bearwolf (I-sa-autch'-be-te-se), Thin Belly (El-la-caus'-se), Good Heart (Uspil-ta-wat'-se), Crazy Head (A-su-ma'-ratz), Bull-goes-hunting, Old Dog, Long Snake, White Mouth, Hunts-his-enemy, Spotted Tail, Red Sides, Small Waist, The Old Crow, Little Lodge, and many others, which in the Crow vernacular are absolutely unpronounceable by a white man. The Indian name for Crow, the name of their tribe, is Ab-sau'-ro-ke, but you cannot express many of their sounds by any written characters, as they are uttered partly down in the throat. It is unlike any language I ever heard spoken before. Some Indians—for instance, the Nez Percés, and others on the Pacific coast—have a pleasant, musical language; but not so with the Crows. I do not know who is the head-chief now of the Crows. I think the chieftaincy of this tribe depends much upon the force of character and ability of the man to draw the people after him.

Crazy Head is smart, but said to be noisy and impulsive; Iron Bull is a wise counselor, and shows an iron constitution and unconquerable will. When he opens his mouth, he speaks as one having authority, and they all give attention. He and Long Horse are good warriors; Good Heart has a very pleasant, good-natured face; while Blackfoot, of tall, portly form and dignified bearing, is intelligent, a good talker, and a shrewd politician, though some of his people say he doesn't fight well.

Blackfoot was the chief spokesman for the Indians in the council, and it is amusing to read some of his speeches, which show no little good sense and shrewdness, with an occasional sparkle of wit. They did not want to sign another treaty, feeling that they had been badly swindled by the council-treaty of Laramie in 1867, asserting that it had neither been explained to them correctly nor carried out in good faith by the Government. They felt that they had been wronged. Then, this was their home, where they were born and reared; where they had long hunted the elk and buffalo ; where the bones of their fathers and mothers now reposed ; and they were loath to leave it.

It may be of interest to the curious to see a specimen of Indian eloquence with the gestures and genuflections left out. After the council had been opened with religious services and Mr. Brunot had explained the object of his visit, speaking through an intepreter, Blackfoot arose and said :

"You call the Great Spirit Jesus in your language; we call him, in the Crow language, E-so-we-wat'-se. I am going to light the pipe and talk to the Great Spirit"—and lighting his pipe and looking up reverently, he said : "The Great Spirit has made the red-man and the white man and sees us all before him to-day. Have pity upon us! May the white man and the Indian speak truth to each other to-day! The sun that looks down upon us to-day, and gives us light and heat, sees that our hearts are true and that all we do is for the good of the poor red-man. The moon that shines upon us in the night-time will see us prosper and do well. The earth on which we walk, from which we come, which we love as our mother, which we love as our country, we ask thee to see that we do that which is good for us and our children. This tobacco comes from the whites; we mix it with bark that comes from the Indian trees and burn it before thee, O Great Spirit! So may our hearts and the hearts of the white men go out before thee and be made good and right !"

As he invoked the Great Spirit, the earth, the moon, and the sun, the pipe was reverently held in the direction of each, after which it was presented to each of the commissioners, then to the chiefs, to smoke, when he said :

"We are here together to-day, the red-men and the white men. We are glad to see you, for we want to have a long talk. There are a great many things we want to say. You came to see us last year, but we were not here; we were away getting buffalo. We were sorry we did not see you, but we were a long way off beyond the mountains and could not come. But this year, when we heard that you were coming, we made haste to come and meet you. We had to cross mountains and rivers; our people were weary and sick, but we wanted to see your face. You are our friends, and we are the white man's friends. We have a large country. We set up our lodge-poles; one reaches to the Yellowstone, the other is on White River, another one goes to the Wind River, and the others are on Bridger Mountains. This is our land. Many of these old Crows you see were born here. Our young men were raised here. Our fathers and mothers are buried here. It is a rich country; the whites are on it, they are stealing our quartz, but we say nothing. They steal a great deal of our money; they kill our buffalo; they go wolfing on our country. We do not want them to go into our country. We want guns and ammunition to fight the Sioux with. We do not want to exchange our land. You are my friend. If I were to go into the white men's country and bloody it as they do our country you would not like it. For many years I have known the whites. You have a big heart, but not so with the white men who come into our country. Some of them never sucked their mothers' breasts. I think they were raised like a buffalo, and sucked a buffalo-cow for their mother. They have no hearts. I was not raised in that way. I am a man. I was raised and sucked milk from my mother's breast. There is no white man's blood on my hands, and I am not ashamed to shake hands with you. What I say is true. I am your friend. The sun sees me and hears what I say. The Great Spirit hears me and knows that it is true. Did I ask these white men to come here and crowd me? Buffalo-robes are my money; we have some buffalo left yet. If I go to the buffalo-country and bring no robes back, the traders will not look at me and say, 'How, how!' as they would if I had plenty. When you go to fight the Sioux, come and tell us. You are afraid of the Sioux. Two years ago I went with the soldiers. They were very brave, and were going through the Sioux country. I wanted to go ahead, but they got scared and turned back. They were the whirlwind. They went toward the Sioux country, but the whirlwind turned back. We are not the whirlwind, but we go to the Sioux and fight them, and do not turn back. But we are not the whirlwind. The Crows and Sioux are at war, but I went into the Sioux camp alone. They offered to give us two hundred and sixty ponies, all taken from the whites, if we would join them. They took me by the arm and wanted me to stay with them and fight the white man, but I pulled loose from them and would not do so.

"You say the railroad is coming up the Yellowstone, that it is like the whirlwind and cannot be turned back. We do not want it to come. I do not think it will come. The Sioux are in the way, and you are afraid of them. They will turn the whirlwind back. When we fight the Sioux, they have better guns than we have. The Crows are the white man's friend, but the Sioux fight the Crows and fight the white men, but you give them better guns than you give us. We do not want you to give them guns and ammunition and blankets."

When Mr. Brunot was reading the treaty made at Laramie, Blackfoot interrupted him and said: "It is all lies. We do not want to hear any more of it. Wrap it up and throw it away. The Indian way of making a treaty is to light a pipe and smoke it. At Laramie the treaty was made. We did not feel right about it. We had made a long journey, and felt tired and sick. They gave us some horses. They thought they were doing a big thing, and making us a big present. But the horses were wild, like the antelope. We caught them with the lasso; they jumped and kicked; we held tight on to them, but they got away from us. We were tired and sick hunting them, and when we got home they were nearly all gone. The commissioners told us we should have food for forty years. They were big men, and not drunk when they told us, but now they will not give it to us. We asked them if we might have the buffalo for a long time. They said, 'Yes,' but that is not written in the treaty. They promised us plenty of goods and food for forty years, plenty for all the Crows. Listen to what I say: we asked, 'Shall we and our children have food for forty years?' They said, 'Yes, yes,' but that is not in the treaty. We told them that there were many bad Indians, but that we would hold on to the hands of the white man. We told them that the Piegans and Sioux had killed the white men, and that they were afraid of them. I asked them to look at us; that we had no guns, and they should not be afraid of us. They said, 'Yes, yes,' but it is not written there. The treaty, you say, bought all of our land north of the Yellowstone. And what do we get for it? I am ashamed about it. We get a pair of stockings, and when we put them on they go to pieces. They get some old shirts and have them washed, and give them to us. We put them on and our elbows go right through them." (Here he went through the motion of putting on a shirt.) "They bring us blankets, and we can blow through them. They send us tin kettles; we go to get water to carry to our lodges; we dip the water, but it all runs out again. That is what we get for our land. Why do they not send us annuity goods? We go to the buffalo-country and get skins; our wives dress them, and we give them to our friends. We give more presents to our white friends than the annuity goods are worth. Our goods are better than those we get, and this is what we get for our lands.

You ask us to tell you what we want. We want Mexican blankets, elk-teeth, beads, eagle-feathers, panther and other skins. We like fine horses and needle-guns. These things are to us what money is to you."

Language and tobacco were both nearly exhausted, when the council broke up without concluding the treaty. The Indians, after much consultation among themselves, at last consented to sign the treaty, each one marching up in turn and saying, "Yes." They will not touch a pen. It is bad luck, they think. Blackfoot's shrewdness as a politician was shown in his refusal to sign the treaty until strongly urged by the young braves to do so. They had refused to recognize the treaty of Laramie, which Blackfoot now said was "all lies," but they cannot complain of him for any consequences of this treaty.

CHAPTER IV.

Indian Habits, Customs, and Beliefs.—Rescue of Two Captive Women.—Peace Policy.—Matrimony lively.—The Arrow vs. the Idea.—Missionaries.—Passing away.

INDIAN character and customs are so familiar to American readers that I need not linger amid their traditions.

They have quite erroneous ideas of the number and power of the whites, and the policy of sending their chiefs and headmen to Washington to see the " Great Father " has proved wise and salutary. They are fond of war, and take great pride in their deeds of prowess. Many of them rival Münchhausen himself in their wonderful stories of personal heroism and courage. They are good story-tellers as well as good fighters. I was highly entertained one day while listening—rather watching, for he talked more with his hands than with his mouth—to an old fellow, worn out in the service, as he told of an encounter with a Cheyenne in a battle on the Big Horn. Though he talked mostly by signs, yet he made me understand where it happened and how it terminated. By the feint of loading and firing his gun he told how he killed the horse, then the rider; and by a dexterous flourish of the huge knife which he drew from his belt he showed how he took off the Cheyenne's' scalp. The sparkle of his eye and the hearty laugh which followed manifested his satisfaction at this the crowning glory of the event.

It is a dishonor for a warrior to lose his scalp; the loss of a brave's scalp dishonors him in the future state. His spirit is in torment, and can never go to the red-man's heaven until a relative or friend avenges his death by taking the scalp of another, no matter who, so it be an enemy, by which it is redeemed and admitted to the "happy hunting-grounds."

They "marry and are given in marriage" according to their custom; each having as many wives as he may desire, provided he has ponies enough to pay for them.

The degradation and servitude of the squaws excite sympathy. What a field for the labors of E. Cady Stanton, Anna Dickinson, Susan B. Anthony, and Mrs. Dr. Mary Walker, in the interest of "woman's rights!" The nineteenth wife has not even the questionable privilege of a divorce from her liege lord. It is an unpardonable crime for a squaw to leave her husband for any cause.

The mother carries her papoose in a kind of pouch or pocket, made of skins and lined with furs, which is fastened to one side of a board, in which the little fellow is placed and bound up so securely, with its back to the board, that it is unable to move hand or foot—straight as the board to which it is lashed. In this condition it is carried, sometimes on the mother's back, and sometimes dangling at the side of the pony. This gives the Indian the straight and erect form in which he takes so much pride.

The large numbers of little papooses form an interesting spectacle as they engage in their youthful sports around the *tepees* or gambol over the grassy plateaus and along the river-banks, strangers to sorrow as well as soap-suds, and happy as they can be. I once thought that they were wanting in affection for their children, but as I have watched an Indian mother caress and fondle her babe so lovingly, and saw how she was delighted as the other little urchins would gather around and kiss and amuse the wee one with their antics, I found that I was greatly mistaken.

The buffalo, or bison, is his principal dependence for food and clothing, in his wild condition, and the hunt his favorite employment. The chase is very exciting, during which the Indian is in his glory. They kill only the fattest ones, then "jerk" the meat to supply them with food for the winter. Of course, they hunt the elk, the deer, the moose, and all other wild animals that are good for food.

Their skill in approaching stealthily upon their game is equaled only by the readiness with which they detect by sight and sound the presence of game or an enemy. Trained from childhood to watch against the approach of foes, the old and cautious will never arise from the ground, no matter how suddenly awakened, until his practised eye has surveyed the field. Or if an enemy is upon him he will know his position before exposing himself above the grass.

The most thrilling of all the scenes of Indian warfare and the most absorbing to American readers are connected with the capture and rescue of American women and girls.

A friend of mine relates an incident of this character which is thrilling indeed. A band of brave men were pursuing a party of Indians, who had stolen their stock while crossing the Plains. They had been out several days, when the scouts discovered a party of Indians camped in a deep ravine in the mountains. By some means they discovered that the savages had three white women-captives. Who they were, how long they had been with the Indians, or of their history, they knew nothing. Nor did it matter. The noble mountaineers determined at once to rescue them, or perish in the attempt. They ascertained the precise location of the camp, surrounded it, and with terrific swoop bore down upon the savages, making the utmost speed to the captives, one of whom was murdered by a squaw at the commencement of the fight. The other two were rescued, while the entire party of Indians, seized with consternation, yet refusing to surrender, were slain. The return of the rescued women to their people, after a long captivity and untold suffering, occasioned the wildest joy. But how many, alas! have been torn by savage hands from home and loved ones, never to return; and how many have been the victims of savage cruelty, until, heart-broken, they have fallen under their burdens, far, far away in this wilderness, to crave death as a precious boon!

Western men, who are most familiar with Indian character and post-tradership corruption, generally denounce in unmeasured terms the present peace-policy of the Government, and recommend the wisdom of turning over all Indian tribes, together with their reservations, to the War Department. And unless there is a great reform in the administration of Indian affairs, such a course appears to be inevitable. The Indians have been robbed of their annuities by traders and officials, furnished with arms and ammunition, and trifled with by the Government so long that, unless there is a change, some fine morning, not in the distant future, the whole country will be appalled by the massacre of all the men in one of these frontier forts, all the inhabitants of one of our beautiful valleys, or an entire detachment of soldiers, with many brave officers, not one escaping to tell the tale, followed by a general Indian war. While the Indians have been mistreated, yet this does not account for all their misdeeds. They are savages by nature, and delight in war and bloodshed. They must be subdued; must be made to feel the strong arm of the Government, and fear it, before they will respect "the powers that be," or before any progress can be made toward their civilization. Let there be a mild but firm government exercised over them. Faithfully observe every treaty, and punish them for every misdemeanor. Then will we have peace throughout our borders, and the Indian will be civilized as far as the possibilities of his nature will permit.

The nomadic life of the Indian in his present condition, if nothing else, defeats all efforts to educate his children. They do not care to have their children learn the manners and customs of the whites. You may teach the *arrow*, but not the *idea*, "how to shoot." If they were compelled to remain on their reservations, the better class of them might be instructed in manual-labor schools, not otherwise.

An estimable gentleman and his wife, of the Methodist Episcopal Church, are at the agency as teachers. They have no power to compel the children to attend school. The children have no kind of inclination schoolward and bookward, and the treacherous little scamps are not easily caught; and yet the catching is before the hanging, even to the alphabet. You can imagine the good woman coaxing a few little dirty urchins in one direction, and the man pursuing two or three fleet boys in another. Finally, they succeed in getting half a dozen or so into the school-room, and, by promising to give each of them a "hard tack," they will stay long enough to repeat the alphabet, and then, with the reward of their learning, the wily young Arabs will scamper off to their sports. One day, in the absence of the teachers, I succeeded in getting about a dozen little urchins into the school-room, and interested them greatly by playing on the melodeon. I put them through various exercises in orthography and arithmetic, then gave them slate and chalk, and it was astonishing how rapidly and accurately they could draw the pictures of various animals, war-scenes, etc.

Some of them are very bright. I was particularly interested in "Goodheart's" two children, a boy and a girl, eight and ten respectively. The chief seemed to take much pains with them, and is delighted with any special attentions they receive from the whites.

Some time since the agent issued an order requiring all white men who had not married squaws to leave the reservation in a given time. For a time matrimony was a lively business. They were "marrying and giving in marriage" until the very day designated for the departure of the incorrigible. Those who were living with squaws, after the Indian custom, were legally married, and those who preferred wedlock to wandering lassoed their ponies and went in search of dusky maidens, who found themselves all at once in great demand; matches were soon made, ponies changed hands, wedding-feasts were numerous, and brides were at a premium. A minister was kept employed, while the red-men rejoiced exceedingly at this accession to their numbers. It was my privilege to witness one of these imposing (!) ceremonies and enjoy the romantic excitement of the occasion.

These Indians are very devout during religious service, as I had occasion to witness on the Sabbath. Indeed, they were more reverent and more readily conformed to the form of worship than many of the whites who were present. To all appearance the missionary field here is white unto the harvest. They listen attentively to the "old, old story of Jesus and his love," and are easily affected to an emotional interest. Their religion, or superstition, embodies the idea of a Supreme Being, the "Great Spirit," and the idea of sacrifice, in the nature of atonement, floats in their traditions. Once a year they go up on a high mountain apart, with ponies to offer in sacrifice to the "Great Spirit" as a kind of atonement for sin. They also worship the sun, moon, and earth. Their "sun-dance" is a kind of morning worship which they observe just at sunrise. The rising sun has always been an object of worship, enjoined by nearly every system of paganism in every age and country.

They have also crude notions of a future state of rewards and punishments, evil spirits, and many other doctrines taught in the Christian Scriptures, which they have received through their traditions, and which they hold very crudely and in connection with their superstitions.

Their "medicine-men," with their lodges, charms, incantations and antic performances, are the products of their belief in evil spirits. The Catholics, Methodists, and Presbyterians, have all been more or less successful in their missionary efforts among the Indians of the West and Northwest, though but little headway has been made in this tribe, as they have never had a regular missionary among them. It will take time and labor to accomplish much among them, but what a reward awaits the self-sacrificing and successful missionary! I was much interested in an account of the death of Rev. Mr. Mitchell, who lived and labored among the Indians of the Indian Territory. He was a member of the Indian Mission Conference of the Methodist Episcopal Church, South, had come to them when they were almost savages, spent his whole life with them, and, when dying, far away from his home and kindred and friends—save his own family—they gathered around him, wept over him, did all they could for him, and when all was over they gave him a Christian burial and moistened his grave with their tears. What a life! what a death! what a funeral! what a monument! In that great day, for which all other days were made, when these dusky children of the forest shall rise up to call him blessed, he, like his Master, "shall see of the travail of his soul and be satisfied."

I was present at one of their night councils. They sat in a

circle upon the ground, with legs crossed and feet under them, all smoking the same pipe, which they passed from one to another, each taking a whiff or two as it went round. In one respect, at least, they differed from the average convention or council among the whites : one talked at a time, and the others listened attentively until he was done. It pleases them greatly for a white man to smoke with them.

As to the object of this council I could get no clew, except that it seemed to concern the internal policy of their tribal government. Well may they counsel together about their municipal affairs and seek to perpetuate their short-lived power, but their doom is as certainly sealed as that civilization will triumph over barbarism. It is only a question of time, and only a brief time at that. What has become of those numerous and powerful tribes formerly occupying the eastern slopes of the continent along the Atlantic seaboard—the Pequods of the Connecticut River, the Narragansetts who had their home on the shores of the magnificent bay that bears their name? Gone, all gone, like a dream of the night, more than a hundred years ago! Where are the Iroquois, the Oneidas, the Tuscaroras, the Senecas, the Hurons, the Mohawks, and all those different tribes that formed that powerful combination known as the confederacy of the "Six Nations?" They have melted away. Where are the Algonquins, who roamed from the Canadas to the Carolinas and were the largest of the eight great Indian families east of the Mississippi River?

The Capitol of the United States now rises in grand proportions where once stood the Indian's wigwam, and its dome pierces the same sky that overarched his villages and his hunting-grounds. He once roamed along the Potomac and the Chesapeake, even to the far-distant shores of Massachusetts and Maine, now the seat of our highest civilization, just as the

Crows and the Sioux traverse the Yellowstone and the Gallatin. And, like the Algonquins, these too will melt away and be forgotten. One fate awaits them all. They have a common nature, a common history, and await a common oblivion. But let us do our duty toward them while they are here.

CHAPTER V.

Up the Yellowstone alone.—Meeting Indians.—Immigrant Gulch.—Wild Mountains.
—Frontier Christians.—The Irrepressible Itinerant Preacher.—Cinnabar Mountain.—Devil's Slide.

AFTER spending several days at the Crow Agency studying Indian character and customs, I returned to the Springs and prepared to pursue my journey up the Yellowstone. The morning of August 21st I bade adieu to my hospitable friend Dr. Hunter, and turned my face westward to find my way alone and on horseback up the Yellowstone to Mammoth Springs, or, in the failure to do that, to return to Bozeman. Hearing that the Crows were in large numbers at the crossing of Shields River, I was quite surprised on reaching the river to find neither lodges nor Indians. The indistinct trail that I was following, the wildness of the scenery, and the thought of the deeds of blood and death committed in sight of the bluffs under the shadow of which I was passing, gave me a little qualmish feeling about the heart, and fired my imagination almost to the point of peopling the quiet, lonely solitude with lurking savages and frightful hobgoblins. The fact that the Sioux and Blackfeet were known to be skulking in the vicinity did not increase my security or courage.

With visions of painted savages floating before me, when about half-way across the little valley, upon looking up the stream to my right, what should I see but six of these denizens of the wilderness all mounted and armed, who, seemingly, had risen up out of the ground, coming in sight so suddenly, and making directly for me! My feelings can better be imagined than expressed. I knew not whether they were Crows or scouts of another tribe. Finding, however, that I could not avoid them, and keeping my eyes open, and my fire-arms in convenient position, ready for the slightest suspicious movement on their part, with all the self-composure I could command, I awaited their approach. I found them to be a party of Crows, one of whom had known me at the agency. After a short powwow, mostly by signs, and after giving the young chief a fish-hook and line for his papoose, we parted on good terms, the last one giving me his hand, with the usual "How" in token of friendship. On my way up the river I met large numbers of them breaking up camp and moving toward the buffalo-country for their fall hunt. They had large numbers of horses, many of which were packed with their camp-equipage, and men, women, and children, were all mounted. They fasten one end of their lodge-poles to the side of the pack-horse, the other end dragging on the ground, making altogether quite a procession as they move along.

I determined to go directly to the Mammoth Hot Springs, where I hoped to meet a party of friends with whom I expected to make a trip to the Geysers; so I continued up the west bank of the river, with Indians on every hand, passing through a rugged, gloomy cañon, overtaking, during the day, a large party of prospecters on their way to the head of Clarke's Fork, where it was reported that rich gold-mines had recently been discovered. Shortly after dark, just as a threatening thunder-cloud and rain-storm were approaching, I heard the barking of a watch-dog, and, observing a glimmering light, rode to it in haste, where I was offered shelter in a humble cabin with a kind family. I turned my horse upon the range, and soon found repose in slumber, for which a lonely ride of fifty miles had given me a relish.

Above the cañon through which we passed is a valley extending up the river to what is known as the Second Cañon of the Yellowstone, fifteen miles distant, and which is from one to three miles wide. Like nearly all of these mountain-valleys, it presents the appearance of having been covered with water. Owing to the numerous beds of small bowlders lying at or near the surface, it cannot be brought fully under cultivation, though there are several choice ranches located in favored spots here and there, producing the cereals and vegetables of a fine quality adapted to this climate. However, it furnishes excellent stock-range, and thousands of head of cattle and horses were grazing in the vicinity. Across the river to the east in a deep gorge, called Immigrant Gulch, is a mining-camp—one of the first discovered in the Territory—containing fifty or seventy-five men, who make from two dollars and a half to ten dollars per day, and are now busily engaged removing huge bowlders and sluicing away great banks of earth and gravel in search of the precious metal deposited there in ages that are past and gone.

The mountains here show abundant evidence of volcanic action, are rugged and lofty, their summits mantled with perpetual snow, giving the scenery quite an interesting and picturesque appearance. Just over there to the east, promiscuously grouped together, is a cluster of cone-shaped peaks, their sides partly darkened with timber for a distance, and carved, by aqueous forces long acting upon them, into dark and gloomy gorges where the sun scarcely ever penetrates, and rising like wonderful pyramids into the heavens, their cloud-bathed summits towering far beyond the timber-line to an altitude of thousands of feet, and which are visible for many miles in every direction. They form part of a range that extends for many miles, from north to south, on that side of the Yellowstone.

The altitude of the valley here is between five and six thousand feet, and the summit of the range about ten thousand, above sea-level.

Contrary to expectation, I found about ten families scattered along the valley, some farming, some gardening, others making butter and cheese, while many were simply watching their herds as they grazed in safety upon the rich meadows. Among them were a number of families late from Oregon with their cattle and horses, only waiting anxiously for the Lower Yellowstone to be opened for settlement. The fame of this country has gone far and wide, and it will doubtless be settled rapidly when the roving bands of Indians are removed, or it is thought safe to venture there.

Little was I expecting to find any religious people, much less members of our own Church, away here in this wilderness; but the events of the day show that I was to be happily disappointed. Learning from the hostess at the breakfast-table that there was a religious family living on the road, who it was thought were Methodists, I determined, if possible, to find them, even if I could not stop long with them. And rest assured, when a Methodist preacher, who has had some experience in traveling over the prairies and mountains of the frontier, hunting up and gathering together the scattered flocks, once gets upon the track of a Methodist family, long must be the distance and dim the trail, if he is not sure of the object of his search! And happy always is the meeting—perhaps in the rude cabin or open tent—and cordial the greeting when the weary itinerant meets with such people. The long distance, the difficult path, the rugged mountains crossed, or rapid streams forded, all are soon forgotten in the refreshing conversation, the family worship, and the generous hospitality extended to him.

It threatened rain, yet I set forward, and on meeting a man

in the road I asked, "Can you tell me where Mr. Strickland lives?"

"Yes, sir; that is my name," he replied.

"Pardon my boldness," said I, "but I have been informed that you are a Christian man. Am I correct?"

"Well, sir, I am trying to be a Christian, though fear that I am quite an unworthy one."

"May I ask if you are a Methodist?"

"I belonged to that Church in Oregon, sir," responded the somewhat astonished man, wondering all the time who his inquisitor could be.

Confident that he was the man I was looking for, and feeling free to make myself known, I remarked, "I am a Methodist minister, and am always happy to meet with Christian people, especially away here in this wilderness." His eyes fairly sparkled as he took my hand and grasped it only as a man could under such circumstances, which was followed by many expressions of joy that came from a warm and happy heart. Then came the invitation—shall I say *command*, for he spoke as one having authority?—to stop at "the cabin," just a mile above. I was not disposed to refuse, as by this time the clouds were growing heavy and the rain beginning to come down. My reception by the good lady of the house was no less cordial, and soon in the small, rude cabin of these mountaineers I felt quite at home and among kind friends, though but a short time before I thought I was indeed a stranger in a strange land, in a wild mountain-country.

Soon it began to rain in earnest, and a large party of tourists on their way to the National Park, who were overtaken in the storm, made their arrival. They were right from the metropolis, and had not fully doffed the attire and conventionalities of city life. They were quite unprepared for such a storm, and it was amusing to see them coming in—old people and young, fashionable gentlemen and fair young belles, on horseback and in buggies, but all eager to find shelter in the hospitable but already crowded cabin, which contained only one apartment. Some were wet, some dry, others frightened and excited, while more than one of the party enjoyed the ludicrous scene. The mother was much worried lest her darling daughters should get a drop of rain upon them; she knew that they would catch their death of cold, and heartily wished they were all back at home. Frilled and fluted aristocracy may shine and shimmer under the gas-light of the city, but may come to grief amid the wild wonders of the West. It was royal fun for the mischievous young brother, who enjoyed such adventures and delighted to tease his "big sisters." The little cabin was crowded, though I have never seen a pioneer's cabin entirely full. Like a stage-coach, it seems to have the happy quality of always containing room for one more. A cheerful fire, however, and a good dinner, together with the repartee that flowed freely, refreshed the spirits of all until the rain ceased, and made it an occasion not to be forgotten.

I found warm friends here, who were from different parts of the States, and whose hospitality I was compelled to share. Some of them had not yet erected houses, but were living in tents; though this renders hospitality no less cordial, or social intercourse less refreshing.

There is a noble-hearted generosity and a freedom from affectation and useless ceremony among these hardy frontiersmen that more than make up for the lack of all the conveniences of a more civilized life.

What a time of refreshing it was to all present, as that evening in the dusky twilight we gathered around the bright campfire in front of the tent for family worship! We read a lesson from the well-worn family Bible by the cheerful fire-light, joined in singing an old familiar air, and then bowed upon the earth, with the starry canopy spread out in beauty above us, and worshiped the God of our fathers and mothers, and invoked his blessings upon us, and his presence with us while exposed to the dangers and hardships of a frontier life. How vividly were the scenes and associations of other days called up! It was a solemn, joyous occasion, and a purer faith was kindled in many hearts. Well might we sing:

> " Blest be the tie that binds
>   Our hearts in Christian love;
> The fellowship of kindred minds
>   Is like to that above.
>
> " Before our Father's throne
>   We pour our ardent prayers!
> Our fears, our hopes, our aims are one,
>   Our comforts and our cares."

My wants being anticipated, and as far as possible supplied, and promising to stop as I returned, I continued my journey up the valley toward the springs, thirty-five miles distant, where we enter the grounds of the National Park. At the head of this valley the road leads through another cañon on the Yellowstone, whose rugged granite walls rise up more than a thousand feet on either side, and the turbid river, compressed to half its natural width, rushes madly through the narrow gorge far below. The road crosses a lofty mountain-spur, passing near the frightful chasm, from which point a splendid view can be obtained. The bright-green color of the water; the numerous ripples upon the surface capped with foam, washing the place where the waves in their madness had dashed against the huge bowlders that had fallen from the walls above; the almost deafening sound of the roaring, rushing torrent, dashing recklessly on like madness itself infuriated; and, besides this, the majestic appearance of the huge rocks piled up on either side to such a stupendous height—all make it a scene strangely impressive and inspiring to behold.

Until recently there was nothing but a bridle-path leading through this gorge, and the traveler was compelled to use great care lest his animal, making but a slight misstep, lose his equilibrium, precipitating him down the fearful chasm to be dashed against the bowlders or thrown into the turbulent waters. However, most of the tourists would be suddenly seized with a mania for walking just here. An unlucky pack-horse did lose his balance, rolling over and over, many feet down the mountain, and would have lost his life but for a friendly feather-bed that was lashed upon his back, which intervened between him and the last rugged bowlder. Such events often happen with packers in the mountains, and frequently prove fatal. A passable wagon-road, however, has been constructed along here now, and extends to the springs.

Passing up the river, about ten miles farther on is what is known as Cinnabar Mountain, the red substance coloring the sides, once thought to be the mineral of this name, showing quite plainly from the road. Near this is observed a wonderful freak of Nature quite similar to a peculiar formation in Weber Cañon on the Union Pacific Railroad, known as "The Devil's Slide." This also has taken the same name, though the one in the Weber dwindles to insignificance compared with this one. Although it is some distance from the road, yet curiosity led us to a closer inspection of this wonderful phenomenon. Numerous ledges of rock, with their ragged edges extending many feet above the surface, traverse the ridge—a spur of the principal range—but the centre of attraction consists of two parallel walls about twenty feet thick, with a space of twenty or thirty feet between them, extending vertically from the base to the summit of the mountain, projecting upward to a height of more than two hundred feet above the surface for a distance of fifteen hundred feet. Their smooth sides, equal height, and erect posture, but for their magnitude, would at first lead you to believe this wonderful formation to be the work of human hands. The rock and earth between the ledges have been worn away by the elements, leaving these immense walls so different from anything around them. Considering the process of their formation, the wonderful forces required to throw them into their present position and form, the centuries of ceaseless and untiring labor of the elements dressing and clearing away the rubbish, they stand as monuments of the power of Him who can do all things, and as objects always calculated to attract the attention and excite the wonder and admiration of the curious traveler.

CHAPTER VI.

A Party of Tourists.—Mountain Transportation.—"Roughing it."—Personal Narrative.—Mammoth Hot Springs.—The Natural Wonder and Beauty of the West.

ON my way up the river I fell in with a very pleasant party, consisting of Major Walker and family; Mr. D. H. Fisk, one of the proprietors of the *Helena Herald;* and Judge Symmes, of the legal fraternity. The party had quite an elaborate outfit for traveling and camping, and were enjoying the trip. They were finely mounted and could travel with speed, but the wagons could not always come up in time for lodging and meals. Such events, so common in the mountains, brought them into great straits, and sometimes taxed their ingenuity to meet the exigencies of the occasion. Before reaching the Mammoth Springs they had to exchange their wagons for pack-animals. This is a method of transportation across mountains and through cañons where wagons cannot go. The pack-saddle is made much like a "saw-buck," with horns sticking up at the four corners to lash the loading to. When the load is all on the animal's back a rope is securely lashed about it and fastened by an ingenious loop known as the "diamond-hitch." In this way all kinds of goods are transported across rugged mountains, turbulent streams, and trackless deserts and forests. The noble animals are soon trained and get well up to their business, avoiding contact with jutting rocks and trees, walking with the utmost cau-

WHITE MOUNTAIN, MAMMOTH SPRINGS.

tion over dangerous precipices where a single misstep would prove disastrous. They will sometimes walk a log—with the top side flattened—across a chasm as steadily and safely as a man! Before they become trained they do not always bring their load into camp "right side up with care." If the pack is insecurely fastened and careens to one side, the animal seems to grow indignant at his master's carelessness, and goes through the gymnastic exercise known as "bucking," seldom satisfied while anything remains upon his back. Sometimes a misstep on a mountain-side hurls him over the rocks and down into a cavern below, possibly landing him in a rushing, roaring torrent. Near the Springs Major Walker's party were packing a little mule on the mountain-side, in which process the ladies were taking a lively interest. The little fellow was not accustomed to this kind of service, and just as the great bulky load was lashed on his back he lost his balance and away he went rolling over and over down the mountain until he reached the bottom of the slope. Being uninjured he regained his feet and climbed up again to the point of departure, much to the delight of the young ladies, who, possibly, were more concerned for their wardrobes than the little mule.

The party mounted and rode across the mountains to the Springs, but their baggage did not come up until the next day. They had to borrow blankets and seek "tired nature's sweet restorer" in quite primitive style. But the hardy tourists already here shared their rude accommodations with them, and the entire party enjoyed "roughing it."

While our friends are here at the Springs, we resume our personal narrative.

After a ride of twelve miles up the west bank of the Yellowstone, crossing several rugged little streams which come dashing down from the snowy heights, and passing miles of sterile country covered with bowlders and sage-brush, interspersed here and there with low grassy valleys and little lakelets swarming with water-fowl, I reached the mouth of Gardiner's River coming in from the southwest, a bold, turbid stream, two-thirds the size of the Yellowstone, in its course leaping over fearful chasms and roaring through gloomy gorges cut in volcanic rocks. Its whirlpools and eddies swarm with beautiful trout. Here the lover of Nature can find much in mountain, river, and valley, to arrest his attention and excite his admiration, while the pleasure-seeker would fain linger at the river-side taking the speckled beauties with hook-and-line.

Following the trail up the west side of this stream, ascending a succession of plateaus and ridges until the summit of a mountain-spur is gained, several hundred feet above the river, I came suddenly out in full view of the far-famed Hot Springs. Having read glowing descriptions of the place, and being rather despondent from the fatigue of travel, I felt somewhat disappointed, and feared my expectations would not be fully met; but all such impressions vanished at first view of the strangely-beautiful scene, and I felt that the half had not been told, though the sun was obscured by clouds, depriving me of much of the inspiration that the first view would otherwise have furnished.

The proprietors of the place, two young gentlemen from Bozeman, anticipating the value of these springs as a place of resort for pleasure-seekers and invalids, had taken possession of them before the passage of the bill including them in the National Park, and styled them the Mammoth Hot Springs. But Dr. Hayden, the United States Geologist, doubtless moved by the first impression made upon his mind on arriving here, gave them the title of White Mountain Hot Springs. Both titles are quite appropriate, considering their mammoth proportions—surpassing anything of the kind yet discovered—and the vast mountain of white and yellowish deposit made from the mineral solutions contained in the immense volumes of water gurgling up from scores of boiling fountains. This immense calcareous formation, with its numberless and intricate phenomena, baffling all attempts at description, is the chief object of interest here. The first impression on beholding it is that of a snowy mountain beautifully terraced, with projections extending out in various directions, resembling frozen cascades, as though the high, foam-crested waves, in their rapid descent over the steep and rugged declivity, were suddenly arrested and congealed on the spot in all their native beauty. There are fifty or sixty of these springs of greater and smaller dimensions, extending over an area of about a mile square; though there are remains of springs of the same kind for miles around, and mountains of the same deposit overgrown with pine-trees, perhaps hundreds of years old. Most of the water is at boiling heat, and contains in solution a great amount of lime, sulphur, and magnesia, with some soda, alumina, and other substances, which are slowly deposited in every conceivable form and shape as the water flows along in its course down the mountain-side.

On each level, or terrace, there is a large central spring, which is usually surrounded by a basin of several feet in diameter, and the water, after leaving the main basin at different portions of the delicately-wrought rim, flows down the declivity, step by step, forming hundreds of basins and reservoirs of every size and depth, from a few inches to six or eight feet in diameter, and from one inch to several feet in depth, their margins beautifully scalloped with a finish resembling bead-work of exquisite beauty. The character of the formation depends upon the temperature and flow of the water, as well as upon the character of prevailing minerals at that particular place. Where the water flows slowly, and with but slight ebullition, the smaller basins and terraces are formed, one below the other, with their delicate partitions and beautifully-fringed borders; and where the volume and momentum are greater, the basins are larger and deeper, and the ornamentation proportionately coarser. Where the water flows quite rapidly, the pools are filling up, leaving the deposit in wave-like forms, just like water congealed when flowing over a cascade. Underneath the sides of many of the basins are beautifully-arranged stalactites, formed by the dripping of the water ; and, by digging beneath the surface at places where the springs are inactive, the most delicate and charming specimens of every character and form can be obtained—stalactites, stalagmites, grottoes, etc., all delicately arranged as the water filtrates through the crevices and perforations of the deposit. The larger pools, before the erection of bathing-houses, afforded a splendid opportunity to enjoy the luxury of bathing, as water of any temperature desirable could be secured. The sides of the mountain for hundreds of yards in extent are covered with this calcareous incrustation, formerly possessing all the ornamental attractions of the springs now in action. It is a scene sublime in itself to see the entire area with its numerous and terraced reservoirs, and millions of delicate little urns, sparkling with water transparent as glass, and tinged with many varieties of coloring, all glistening under the glare of a noonday sun. But the water is constantly changing its channel, and atmospheric agencies have disfigured much of the work, leaving a great portion of it only the resemblance of an old ruin.

Every active spring or cluster of springs has its succession of little urns and reservoirs extending in various directions. The largest spring now active, situated about half-way up the mountain on the outer edge of the main terrace, has a basin about twenty-five by forty feet in diameter, in the centre of which the water boils up several inches above the surface, and is so transparent that you can, by approaching the margin, look down into the heated depths many feet below the surface. The sides of the cavern are ornamented with a coral-like formation of almost every variety of shade, with a fine, silky substance, much like moss, of a bright vegetable green, spread over it thinly, which, with the slight ebullition of the water keeping it in constant motion, and the blue sky reflected in the transparent depths, gives it an enchanting beauty far beyond the skill of the finest artist. Here all the hues of the rainbow are seen and arranged so gorgeously that, with other strange views by which one is surrounded, you almost imagine yourself in some fairy region, the wonders of which baffle all attempts of pen or pencil to portray them.

Besides the elegant sculpturing of this deposit, imagine, if you can, the wonderful variety of delicate and artistically-arranged colors with which it is adorned. The mineral-charged fluid lays down pavements here and there of all the shades of red, from bright scarlet to rose-tint, beautiful layers of bright sulphur-yellow, interspersed with tints of green—all elaborately arranged in Nature's own order. Viewed from the Tower Creek trail, which passes at the base, this section of the mountain has a very architectural appearance.

But descending the mountain from which we first beheld the springs, and where we left the reader, we come to the first level, or terrace, the base of the principal formation. There are several springs, the water of which is used by the scores of invalids already flocking here to be healed of their maladies. Here, also, are the small bath-houses erected by the proprietors, for the use of which a handsome sum is generally exacted. The medicinal properties of each fountain seem to be different, and the invalid can use that best adapted to his case. Just over there to our right, in the mouth of a little gorge, coming down from the mountain, by the side of the sparkling brook of snow-water, among the pine-trees, where the smoke is curling up from many fires, are the camps of the tourists and invalids who have come hither, and are abiding in rudely-constructed cabins, some in tents, enjoying all the luxuries of camp-life. Rather a motley, though quite a lively, group. Some remarkable cures have been effected here, mostly of diseases of the skin, and rheumatism. But I think that the invigorating mountain-air and the healthful influence of camp-life have much to do with many cures that are effected, as these are known to be wonderful remedies in themselves for many of the ills which flesh is heir to.

Here we found many of our friends, who received us kindly, and, with our genial friend W. H. Risk acting as guide and traveling companion, we start out to make the rounds. The first object that excites our curiosity is an old chimney or crater on the first level, composed of the same material abounding here, which some think is the remains of an extinct geyser; though I am inclined to think it was formed by the constant flowing of the water along a certain channel, creeping through this one aperture, forming the deposit around it, raising it higher and higher until the summit of the crater was on a level with the source of that particular fountain, or the fountain was by other means turned from its course. It is quite remarkable, is about twenty feet in diameter, and fifty feet high. The top is shaped like a cone, and on the summit is a funnel-shaped crater. The outward crust resembles the layers of a thatched roof, caused by the flow of the mineral-charged water down the sides. It is called "Liberty-Cap." There are a number of these craters of smaller dimensions, on the rim of the next terrace above, one of which is styled the "Beehive," which was built in the same manner.

As we continue up the mountain, over the remains of inactive springs, we find ourselves wading through beds of magnesia nearly as fine as flour, and traversing places where almost pure pulverized sulphur could be obtained in wagon-loads. Full of curiosity, we applied a match to a bank of it, and found that it would burn freely, but fearing the consequences, and having an antipathy for fire and brimstone anyhow, we made haste to extinguish it.

The formation abounds in crevices and fissures, caused, perhaps, by the settling of the deposit, forcing the springs often to change their channel. Farther back on the mountain are several oblong mounds which invariably contain fissures, through the centres of which are often found delicate crystals of sulphur of rare beauty, formed by the steam and gases emitted from the seething caldrons below.

Certain portions of the mountain also abound in caverns which were once the scene of boiling reservoirs. One of these has been partly explored, and is known as the "Devil's Kitchen;" but, meeting at the entrance a volume of the warm, sickening atmosphere, I desisted from further explorations. It was a gloomy, dismal place, and we could see little bats flitting to and fro, after the stones that we dropped in. In one of these caverns I saw the skeleton of a young deer or elk, which, in its playful gambols, had gone too near and fallen in and perished.

As one first enters the locality of these thermal activities, he hesitates to venture near the margin of the springs; but, finding it generally solid, he soon becomes emboldened, and is in danger of growing too reckless, and may venture too far. At one place we could hear the internal rumbling of the troubled waters rushing along right beneath our feet; and, remembering an opening we had seen in the crust in a dry place where a man had fallen in, we almost shuddered as we thought of the fatal results of a break through here. On one occasion, in company with a friend, while taking a horseback-ride, we ventured upon what we thought to be a solid bed, but what proved to be a treacherous formation, when my friend's horse broke through, burying him up to his sides in what proved to be a bed of dry pulverized magnesia. After a few flounders, horse and rider were again on *terra firma*, and we continued our journey.

The stalactites, and various ornamentations found about the little reservoirs, under the surface, and in the caves and fissures, make beautiful specimens for a cabinet, and have been carried away in vast quantities, though it is forbidden now, as it disfigures the work so much. Beautiful specimens are also obtained by placing little baskets, frames, and other objects of mechanical genius in the water, where in a short time they become incased in a snow-white crust of rare beauty.

The physical causes at work in this region are truly wonderful. Where the vast amount of material comes from, how it is decomposed, brought hither and arranged in the ten thousand wonderful forms it has taken, and how long this work has been in progress, are questions that arise in the mind, but which we leave for others to discuss. Just below the large spring above described is a grove of good-sized pines nearly buried in the sediment, while back of this, up the mountain-side where abound the caves and fissures we mentioned above, not a half-mile away, are trees a hundred years old, growing on the same formation. Known unto the Great Architect, and to him only, are all his works. His ways are past finding out.

This place is now visited every year by hundreds of people. There was no hotel when we were there, though the gentlemanly proprietors will do all they can for the comfort and pleasure of their visitors. As lumber had to be sawed at first with a whipsaw, houses are scarce. I preached on Sunday to a clever and very attentive audience, who seemed to appreciate the services. However, pleasure-resorts are not the most favorable places to make religious impressions.

CHAPTER VII.

The National Park.—Tower Falls.—Old Castles.—Bold Adventure.—Devil's Hoof.—
Rare Jewels.—Petrifaction.

THE Mammoth Springs are seventy miles from Bozeman, and just across the line in Wyoming Territory, in the northeastern corner of the National Park. A recent act of Congress set apart and dedicated a vast area of this marvelous country, fifty-five by sixty-five miles in extent, embracing the sources of the Missouri, the Yellowstone, and the Snake Rivers, as a national park. The conception was a happy one, and the wisdom of the Government in thus providing for the curiosity-hunters and the lovers of the wonderful will be appreciated by all the generations to come. No country in the world of the same extent contains half the natural curiosities or one tithe the wonderful freaks and marvelous formations of Nature which excite to so large a degree the admiration and wonder of the savage and the *savant*, the unlettered and the learned. Its mountains are higher and bolder; its gorges are deeper and darker, its cañons grander and gloomier, its cataracts more beautiful, its scenery sublimer, its volcanic phenomena more marvelous, its geysers more numerous and grander, and its contrasts and characteristics more varied and vivid, than can be found in any other quarter of the globe. Even now the health and pleasure seekers of the Great West gravitate toward the National Park, in which wheels are a nuisance and pack-animals are in demand. Already quite a thriving business is done by packmen who keep a supply of pack mules and horses on hand for the accommodation of tourists. It is surprising how much these pack-animals can carry, and with what dexterity they can be loaded and unloaded. The packmen also act as guides, and for the twofold service they demand good wages. This mode of traveling becomes quite fascinating and exhilarating when one gets accustomed to it, and the round trip is made delightful and profitable, as well as heathful.

The journey through the National Park will well repay the philosopher and the scientist, as well as the mere wonder-seeking tourist. The marvelous freaks and phenomena of Nature scattered over this area await the solutions of science and the revelations of philosophy.

All things ready, I started on Monday, August 25th, alone, expecting soon to rejoin the party who had started the evening before. Crossing Gardiner's River and following up the east fork, I passed a beautiful cascade to the right and a high mountain on the left, its sides ribbed with huge basaltic columns standing boldly and grandly up to view. Following the intricate meanderings of the trail, and passing the place where my party had camped, I soon came out into an undulating prairie-country, abounding with rich grass, lovely flowers, and dotted with frequent groves of pine and aspen covered with rich foliage, with now and then a delightful little lakelet nestled between the mountains. But here, alas! with all my caution, I lost the trail, and, bearing too far to the right, wandered in anxious solicitude, very much disliking the prospect of spending a night alone in this wild solitude without food or shelter, and with nothing but the wild beasts of the forest for companions. But hurrying forward in the general course over mountain and valley, I soon struck a trail, though not positive that it was the right one; and just before nightfall, and as a dark, threatening thunder-cloud was fast gathering overhead, to my great relief I beheld, from the verge of a lofty precipice—where I had climbed to gain a momentary view of a peculiar freak of Nature in a gorge below—the smoke from the camp-fires curling up through the tops of the pines in a little grove on the opposite side of Tower Creek, where the party had camped for the night.

Here a rugged, swiftly-running little stream, dashing along over huge bowlders, and environed by rugged, dismal walls, comes down from a high ridge to the west, through a gloomy gorge made more dismal by the dense, overshadowing pines. Only a few hundred yards before its entrance into the Yellowstone, as if jubilant at the prospective release from its prison-walls, at one bound it leaps over a perpendicular precipice of one hundred and fifty-six feet, making one of the most beautiful little waterfalls I had ever beheld. It is called Tower Falls. The softer substances on the sides of the cañon are worn away by the elements, leaving numberless columns of volcanic breccia of every size and form, from ten to fifty feet high, standing like old castles and lofty towers, or sending up their slender forms like domes of churches or the spiral minarets of heathen temples. One is carried back to the days of chivalry and knighthood, and imagines that before him is the lordly castle of some ancient hero, now robbed of its beauty and glory by the ruthless elements and the ravages of time, with these immense columns standing as sentinels guarding the sacredness of the place.

The many bright, blending colors—all the shades of red, brown, yellow, and green—with which the rock-walls of the cañon and the shelly columns are decked, and the numerous fantastic shapes of the capricious formations, together with the

TOWER FALLS.

noise of the rushing waters, make this an interesting place, and the traveler is tempted to make a longer stay and a closer inspection of its blended beauties. On either side of the falls are two of these immense towers, standing like pillars at the gates of a walled city, or columns at the entrance of some grand cathedral, the crystal waters bounding between them, and spreading out below like a sheet of silvery vapor. With some exertion, I scrambled out to the narrow, crumbling summit of one of these shelly columns and gazed into the foaming chasm full two hundred and fifty feet below, which feat requires a steady head and no little nerve, but amply compensates for the laborious effort. From the mouth of the stream I also, with some difficulty, ascended the gloomy gorge, filled with fallen trees and enormous bowlders, against which the mad waves dashed with foaming fury, until I stood at the very foot of the fall, where my clothes were soon moistened by the rising spray, and obtained a view of the scene that was far more imposing and beautiful. Near the cataract is a huge mass of *débris*, doubtless precipitated from the walls above. It was a clear, calm, summer afternoon; the sun was dropping behind the tall pines on the western mountain, and the rising shadows reminding us of the close of day. Inspired by the surroundings, I lingered long in that retired chamber alone, meditating upon the wonderful works of Nature; and as I watched the water descending in jets and crystal showers, and listened to its hushed murmur, subdued to softness by the overhanging cliffs and towering pines, I could but admire the modestly beautiful little cataract hid away in this lonely yet lovely solitude, where it would not be observed by the curious hundreds passing near, and I returned to camp feeling myself a better man, and meditating upon the greatness, wisdom, and goodness of Nature's God.

From the bank of the river near this place we have a good

view of the mouth of Grand Cañon. On the sides of the walls are evidences of the existence of a strong sulphurous compound, and the cañon has a bright-yellow tinge. Also, at various points along the bank, small springs of sulphur-water ooze out from the wall, giving off a bubbling, frying sound, and filling the air in the vicinity with an offensive sulphurous odor. Observing the bubbling in a channel of a stream of cold water, curiosity tempted me to test the temperature by immersing my hand, for which foolish act I was severely punished, it being at boiling heat, though surrounded by cold water and coming up right through it.

One of the singular formations near Tower Falls, owing to its fancied resemblance, I suppose, to the historic "cloven foot," has been called "Devil's Hoof," while the dismal gorge above, for miles reminding one so forcibly of the land of darkness, is known as the "Devil's Den." It is remarkable that so many of the curious freaks of Nature in the mountains are dedicated to some part of the person or dominion of that distinguished individual, though partly accounted for in the fact that many of these startling appellations were suggested by the old mountaineers and trappers who first explored these regions, and who were familiar with, and quite lavish in the use of, such titles. Every oddly-formed rock or mound, every river, gorge, and glen, having even a fancied likeness to the hideous person whom they had been taught from their infancy to dread, and the regions which they had been warned to shun, received a name fully indicative of the diabolism symbolized. Such a country as this is surely quite suggestive to such minds, and it appears that in many instances the late explorers have followed suit.

We now enter a region abounding in precious stones of various kinds, such as agates, amethysts, sardonyx, chalcedony, malachite, etc. Here, also, are quantities of silicified, petrified, and agatized wood, some of which is very fine and quite wonderful. There are some instances of perfectly-formed standing trees of pure petrifaction. But the best place for securing specimens is at Specimen Mountain, some ten miles east of here, where many varieties of precious and beautifully-formed stones have been found. At that place there are great masses, much resembling the trunks and limbs of trees, the outside of which is almost pure agate, interspersed with well-defined marks like the rings of growth in a tree, while the inside (they being hollow) is beautifully lined with diamond-shaped crystals, some clear, and others tinted with a bright-purple hue. I saw many of the specimens, which are remarkably beautiful.

While at Tower Falls we had rare sport taking the fine speckled trout that throng the eddies in the river. Abundance of game—bear, elk, and deer—exists in the surrounding mountains, but we could not stop to hunt. However, the fir-timber in places was alive with flocks of mountain-grouse, a fowl much resembling a prairie-chicken, though smaller, which afforded fine sport for those of our party who had fowling-pieces. They are easily taken, and when well cooked are very delicious.

Leaving the falls in the afternoon, our trail bore to the right and wound up a long, barren ridge, with rolling hills of beautiful meadows, dotted with woodlands on our left, and vast forests of pine, penetrated by Tower Cañon, on our right. When about half-way up to the summit of Mount Washburn, the main trail veers still farther to the right through the dense pine-timber; thence southward, crossing the rim of the basin just west of the mountain to the Great Falls and Grand Cañon of the Yellowstone.

CHAPTER VIII.

Mount Washburn.—Sublime Scenery.—Grand Cañon.—Upper Falls.—Perilous Position.—Great Falls.

MOUNT WASHBURN, so named by a party of explorers led by General H. D. Washburn, in 1870, rises to the remarkable altitude of ten thousand four hundred and eighty feet, barometrical measurement, above the level of the sea. Its summit may be reached on horseback, though with difficulty.

Standing four hundred feet above the line of perpetual snow, and overlooking the lesser and lower peaks which surround it, the view of the surrounding country, for from fifty to one hundred miles in every direction over this wonderland of America, is unsurpassed. The eye surveys the very "crown of the continent," where the great rivers, the Columbia, the Colorado, and the Missouri, in miniature streamlets, interlap each other, and whence, fed by eternal snows, they leap and plunge down the rough and rocky defiles to the fertile valleys below, increasing in volume as they flow to every point of the compass, until they are lost in the two great oceans of the world. The course of the river can be distinctly traced to its source in Yellowstone Lake.

From the summit, or even from a position far up the sides, with a good field-glass, can be distinctly seen the main summit of the Rocky Mountains, to the south and west, the great water-

CLIFFS ON THE YELLOWSTONE.

the world." From those snow-crowned heights, according to an ancient legend, the Blackfoot can look over into the happy hunting-grounds, with its enchanting lakes and rivers, its delightful landscapes, balmy breezes, and unclouded sun, the abode of departed and happy spirits who have crossed over the mystic river, where their enemies can never come, and where they can chase the antelope, elk, and buffalo, forever. At our feet, to the east, can be easily traced the outlines of the Grand Cañon extending for twenty miles down the river from the falls, its rugged walls forbidding at every point a descent to the bottom without great effort and no little danger. Then stretching away, in every direction, is one vast area of pine-forest, as far as the eye can reach, with only a small opening here and there, darkening the sides of the mountains, and mantling the tablelands and undulating hills between with a covering of green. Surely such a view is grand beyond description. Considering the wild nature of the yet only partially explored country, the wonders that meet the eye at every turn, and the exquisite beauty of the broad and variegated landscape as it is revealed in such a pure, transparent atmosphere, the view is rich with compensation, and inspiring to the lover of the sublime in Nature.

We find ourselves lost in contemplation, and the mind is completely overwhelmed as it tries to grapple with the momentous subjects presented. We are not far from the very crest of a vast continent, and can almost look down upon the sources of some of the grandest rivers of the globe, whose waters, starting yonder in those heaven-born fountains, go forth to every land to bless the nations of the earth. See that inland sea there, sleeping near the very top of the continent, and that vast basin which was once an inland ocean! Only think of the time when these mountains were fiery volcanoes, darkening the heavens with their smoke, and pouring their fiery lavas into the hissing and tossing waters, already troubled by subterranean throes and internal fires bursting forth in their midst, their mad waves beating high upon the rocky shores! Then the long ages of ceaseless action and patient effort, during which the lake has been partly drained by the cutting out of the Grand Cañon, and the volcanoes have been robbed of their fury! Even yet the fiery demon below the surface reminds us of his spent fury, and departing glory, by the fearful concussions and grand eruptions, as volumes of boiling water are hurled hundreds of feet into the air.

But I must hasten on to join our party, who have again left me alone on the mountain. I find them camped just at the southern base of Washburn, by a rippling brook in the shade of the trees near a lovely park where we spend a pleasant night.

Just down the stream on which we camped, a short distance to our left, is another group of boiling springs, the sulphurous fumes of which scented the air where we were camped. We were satisfied with a description, and the offensive odors coming from that direction, and did not visit them. The greenish-yellow, paint-like fluid, and the sulphurous slime, the noisy ebullition, the sickening, suffocating fumes emitted, and the desolate and unearthly appearance of the place, tempted the explorers to draw upon the infernal vocabulary again, and they styled the place "Hell-Broth Springs."

Breakfast over, the horses brought in, saddled, and everything packed up, at an early hour we left camp, and, after a ride of some ten miles down the general course of a little stream, our trail following a zigzag route to evade the fallen timber and a dense forest of pines, we came to the Great Falls, at the head of the Grand Cañon of the Yellowstone River. This place is of great interest to the tourist, where he will be tempted to tarry long amid the wondrous grandeur and beauty of scenes which even the finest linguist must ever fail to describe and the most skillful artist despair of painting, the eye being the only medium through which a just conception of the surpassing beauty and sublimity of the place can be obtained. The river, after flowing through a beautiful, meadow-like valley, thence winding gently along under the shade of a lovely woodland, with placid and steady current, the water so clear that the fish can be seen in their sports along the bottom, the vegetation coming to the water's edge on either side, with no warning save two small rapids just above the brink, is compressed to one hundred and fifty feet in width, and drops over a precipice of one hundred and forty feet. A quarter of a mile below it is again narrowed between two great walls, and makes a fearful bound over a perpendicular shelf into the spray-filled chasm three hundred and fifty feet in depth, attended with a fearful, rushing sound that may be heard for miles—making five hundred feet of perpendicular fall within a distance of a few hundred yards! Then away in the "dizzy distance," far, far below us, the stream is seemingly narrowed to a brook, looking more like an emerald-tinted ribbon than a mighty, roaring river, and dashes on with the velocity of a torrent, rushing down steep declivities and spinning around short angles, the furious waves wasting their puny strength against the massive walls of the Grand Cañon, in the gloomy depths of which the river disappears until it issues from the fearful gorge at the mouth of Tower Creek, many miles below.

The Upper Falls, though they are not so high, yet, being nearer the surface of the ground among the pines and exposed to the sunlight, which adds greatly to their beauty, and being easy of access from every point, are quite picturesque. Part way down the chasm the volume strikes a second ledge—a sort of bench—which ruffles the smooth surface, lashing the water into foam which descends in jets and showers with a sort of

THE UPPER FALL, YELLOWSTONE.

LOWER FALLS, YELLOWSTONE.

ricochet or glancing movement, sending up a cloud of spray all sparkling with crystal brightness in the sunlight, the beauty made more enchanting by the bright rainbows that glitter in the vapor. One can stand upon the very brink of the precipice, and also descend to the foot, where he will soon be drenched with spray. In the presence of such wonders, hours seemed like moments; and from a rock protruding nearly midway over the cataract, almost forgetting that I was alone, long after our party had gone, I sat watching the descending waters, listening to the song of the cataract, and admiring the lovely rainbows playing upon the snow-white vapor, reluctant to depart, and regretting the shortness of my stay.

But the Lower Falls, owing to their stupendous height and their imposing and gorgeous surroundings, constitute the centre of attraction. You can descend to the very brink of the fearful precipice, and, with steady nerve, can peer into the seething abyss below. From this point you obtain the best view of the cañon, though the best place to view the falls is from one of the overhanging cliffs in the cañon farther down the stream.

The cañon commencing at the upper cataract is here fully two thousand feet above the bed of the stream, its almost vertical sides carved by the aqueous forces and atmospheric agencies into towers, turrets, domes, castles, spiral columns, and deep caverns and chambers of all shapes and dimensions, of great architectural beauty, the Gothic columns and vast escarpments all gorgeously arrayed in lively colors of almost every conceivable hue, beautifully blending into each other, showing the handiwork of a skillful architect and artist.

Looking down the river, the vast gorge increases in depth, and from its gray, shelving summits fringed with pines, or its bold promontories, you can peer into the awful depths below filled with clouds of rising spray, and made lively by the echo of the mighty torrent and the rush of maddened billows. The mind is overwhelmed with the grandeur and marvelous beauty of the scene, and completely captivated by the irresistible fascinations of the place, with its weird surroundings, so unlike anything ever seen before. We lingered here nearly a whole day on our return; and, on making the descent to the water's edge below, we obtained a view with a glass from almost every point of observation.

The fall, at first sight, does not look so high as you expected, yet it is marvelously grand, presenting the appearance of a symmetrical and unbroken sheet of snow-like foam, or silver tapestry suspended from the colossal pillars above, set in dark masses of rock, on either side forming a beautiful background, and disappearing in a cloud of ascending spray which is tinged with mellow sunlight and gorgeously colored with brilliant rainbows. Says Mr. Langford, one of the first explorers: "A grander scene than the lower cataract of the Yellowstone was never witnessed by mortal eyes. The volume seemed to be adapted to the harmonies of the surrounding scenery. Had it been greater or smaller it would have been less impressive. The river, from a width of two hundred feet above the fall, is compressed by converging rocks to one hundred and fifty feet where it takes the plunge. The shelf over which it falls is as level as a work of art. The height by actual line-measurement is three hundred and fifty feet. It is a sheer, compact, solid, perpendicular sheet, faultless in all the elements of picturesque beauty." The rocks on either side, moistened constantly by the spray, are beautifully adorned with vegetation and many-tinted mosses. I observed on the opposite bank of the river, overshadowed by the pine-crested wall, keeping out forever the rays of the sun, a bank of snow which perhaps remains in its secluded retreat from year to year. On the very brink of the precipice, peering over the dizzy depths, I plucked a sprig of evergreen, and from a crevice in the wall gathered a bouquet of flowers as relics of the delightful visit.

A perpendicular chasm of several hundred feet, commencing at the fall and extending three or four hundred yards below, makes the descent to the cataract on this side impossible; though one man claims to have descended on the opposite side to the very foot of the fall. Feeling strong and being full of adventure, I determined, if possible, to make the descent and explore the tunneled walls to the very bottom of the cañon; and, after several unsuccessful attempts, in company with my friend W. H. Todd and two other gentlemen, with great effort we succeeded in making the descent of the fearful gorge down to the water's edge, a few hundred yards below the falls, a feat that requires a steady head and all the nerve and muscle that a strong man and an expert and careful climber can command, and which is attended with no little danger. This, however, we did not realize until far down the cañon, nor fully appreciate until our return. The thought of it makes me almost shudder to this very moment.

From a lofty eminence we survey what seems to be a plausible route, and armed with strong staves and stout hearts we make the dangerous adventure. Down, down, down we go, taking a zigzag course, now crouching 'neath shelving, overhanging rocks, now digging footholds in the clay or brittle wall along the side of some steep acclivity, or clambering carefully along the shelving and treacherous summit of a dark, yawning chasm right below, as if opening to receive us. The detached fragments of rock set in motion by us go thundering down the frightful gorge, and seem to echo back the fate of him who, losing his balance or missing his frail foothold, should be precipitated into the gloomy depths. But, choosing well our footing, and following an angular course, with the exception of one incident that came near proving fatal, we reached the bottom in safety. I was leading the van, and, feeling confident that we could follow the little gulch we were in to the bottom, all were going at good speed and we became careless in looking out the path ahead, when, what was my surprise all at once to find myself right on the verge of a precipice, over which if I plunged I would lose my balance, and be dashed into a thousand pieces! The surface below was too smooth and steep to stand upon, and with the momentum gained going over the "jump-off" I would be precipitated down the gorge. But here another difficulty arose: while I could scarcely hold my footing where I was, the surface was so smooth that I could not move backward one inch; and if my friends above me moved from their places, the vast beds of talus around them would be set in motion and send me over the cliff. What was to be done? I was inching downward, and six inches more would doubtless tumble me down the gulf. The roar of the water was so great that I could not communicate with my friends, who, seeing my dilemma, sat motionless (save the one in the rear, who started to my relief), the best thing they could do. Keeping quite "cool," and planting my staff in a shallow niche below on the side-wall, with my knife I picked a frail foothold in the shelly rock, regaining my footing, and I soon scrambled out, when I was joined by my companions, who, by-the-way, were frightened far more than myself; and choosing a circuitous route we were soon at the very bottom of the Grand Cañon beside the foam-crested waves of the Yellowstone, and felt amply compensated for the effort, in the sublimity of the surrounding scenery. Proudly we walked along the banks of the river and slaked our thirst from the emerald-tinted stream, feeling that we were explorers in this region, and the first to set foot upon these mystic shores.

The view from the bottom of the cañon is grand and imposing in the extreme. The river no longer appears as the little silvery streamlet moving smoothly along its winding bed, as seen from the summit in the distance, but a foaming, dashing torrent, more than a hundred feet wide, its raging billows lashed into foam as they beat high upon the solid rocks. The tall, stately pines at the top of the cañon appeared to be but dwarfed shrubs, while our companions whom we left behind, standing upon the promontory above us, looked to be but little boys. I never can forget my visit there, and the inspiration of what I believe to be the grandest and most soul-inspiring scene in the National Park. Mud-volcanoes and boiling springs may fade from memory, noisy, spouting geysers cease to attract, but the strangely bewitching beauty and sublimity of this scene, the overpowering sense of the presence of Deity which it gives, will make it an event to which I will always revert with profound gratitude. As we stood in the depths of that vast chamber, and looked up at the towering walls so exquisitely carved, and all decked in lively colors of richest hue, blending together in a manner gorgeous beyond the conception of any artist, arched over with the blue canopy, the bright rays of the sun bathing the whole with mellow light, then cast our eyes up to the grand cataract above, pouring over the fearful precipice, and listened to the tremendous roar of the water descending into the seething abyss, together with the rushing sound of the foam-crested waves dashing madly by as if hastening from the awful scene, we were awed into silence and reverence, feeling that we were in the very antechamber of the great God of Nature, and that he was talking to us and teaching us lessons of his greatness, his grandeur, and his glory, that human language must ever fail to express. A sense of the awful pervades the mind, and we almost felt that we were trespassing upon sacred ground.

and following an angular course, with the exception of one incident that came near proving fatal, we reached the bottom in safety. I was leading the van, and, feeling confident that we could follow the little gulch we were in to the bottom, all were going at good speed and we became careless in looking out the path ahead, when, what was my surprise all at once to find myself right on the verge of a precipice, over which if I plunged I would lose my balance, and be dashed into a thousand pieces! The surface below was too smooth and steep to stand upon, and with the momentum gained going over the "jump-off" I would be precipitated down the gorge. But here another difficulty arose: while I could scarcely hold my footing where I was, the surface was so smooth that I could not move backward one inch; and if my friends above me moved from their places, the vast beds of talus around them would be set in motion and send me over the cliff. What was to be done? I was inching downward, and six inches more would doubtless tumble me down the gulf. The roar of the water was so great that I could not communicate with my friends, who, seeing my dilemma, sat motionless (save the one in the rear, who started to my relief), the best thing they could do. Keeping quite "cool," and planting my staff in a shallow niche below on the side-wall, with my knife I picked a trail foothold in the shelly rock, regaining my footing, and I soon scrambled out, when I was joined by my companions, who, by-the-way, were frightened far more than myself: and choosing a circuitous route we were soon at the very bottom of the Grand Cañon beside the foam-crested waves of the Yellowstone, and felt amply compensated for the effort, in the sublimity of the surrounding scenery. Proudly we walked along the banks of the river and slaked our thirst from the emerald-tinted stream, feeling that we were explorers in this region, and the first to set foot upon these mystic shores.

VIEW FROM THE BOTTOM OF THE CAÑON.

The view from the bottom of the cañon is grand and imposing in the extreme. The river no longer appears as the little silvery streamlet moving smoothly along its winding bed, as seen from the summit in the distance, but a foaming, dashing torrent, more than a hundred feet wide, its raging billows lashed into foam as they beat high upon the solid rocks. The tall, stately pines at the top of the cañon appeared to be but dwarfed shrubs, while our companions whom we left behind, standing upon the promontory above us, looked to be but little boys. I never can forget my visit there, and the inspiration of what I believe to be the grandest and most soul-inspiring scene in the National Park. Mud-volcanoes and boiling springs may fade from memory, noisy, spouting geysers cease to attract, but the strangely bewitching beauty and sublimity of this scene, the overpowering sense of the presence of Deity which it gives, will make it an event to which I will always revert with profound gratitude. As we stood in the depths of that vast chamber, and looked up at the towering walls so exquisitely carved, and all decked in lively colors of richest hue, blending together in a manner gorgeous beyond the conception of any artist, arched over with the blue canopy, the bright rays of the sun bathing the whole with mellow light, then cast our eyes up to the grand cataract above, pouring over the fearful precipice, and listened to the tremendous roar of the water descending into the seething abyss, together with the rushing sound of the foam-crested waves dashing madly by as if hastening from the awful scene, we were awed into silence and reverence, feeling that we were in the very antechamber of the great God of Nature, and that he was talking to us and teaching us lessons of his greatness, his grandeur, and his glory, that human language must ever fail to express. A sense of the awful pervades the mind, and we almost felt that we were trespassing upon sacred ground.

I felt like baring the head and bowing the knee to One who could pile up rocks in such stupendous majesty, and carve and paint them in such matchless splendor, "who cutteth out rivers among the rocks;" "who holdeth the waters in the hollow of his hand," and spreadeth them out in such grandeur and beauty. "Great and marvelous are thy works, Lord God Almighty. Heaven and earth are full of thy glory."

I thought, while I lingered there, if such slight glimpses into the ways and works of Nature's God as are manifest here below, obtained as they are with so much effort, and where at best we must needs "see through a glass darkly," are so overpowering and inspiring to the soul, what must it enjoy when, freed from this cumbersome tenement, and with enlarged capacities, expanded and unobstructed vision, it shall behold with eyes undazzled the beauty of our God, and revel amid the untold glories of that "temple not made with hands, eternal in the heavens."

We left our cards in the crevice of a rock, and, each man taking a pebble from the stream as a souvenir of the visit, we clambered up the rocky steep, which feat was almost as perilous as, and even more difficult than, the descent. We were gone five hours, and all felt it to be one of the most remarkable adventures of a lifetime.

A visit to the National Park is incomplete without a view of the Grand Cañon and Great Falls of the Yellowstone.

GREAT CAÑON OF THE YELLOWSTONE.

CHAPTER IX.

Dr. Hayden's Theory of the Falls and Cañon.—Lost again.—Camp on the Yellowstone.—Sulphur Mountain.—Mud-Volcano.—Giant's Caldron.—Muddy Geyser.—Diabolical Appearance of Everything.

DR. HAYDEN'S theory of this great waterfall and stupendous chasm on the Yellowstone is that the basin around it was once the scene of an immense lake, which in time became the centre of great volcanic activities, erupting vast quantities of lava, which, cooling under water, took the form of basalt, volumes of volcanic ashes and fragments of rock being thrown out from time to time from the craters, forming breccia as it sank through the water and mingled with deposits from siliceous springs.

In course of time the lake was drained away by the cutting out of the cañon. The easily-eroded breccia along the course of the river was cut deeper and deeper as ages rolled on, while springs and creeks and atmospheric agencies combined to carve the sides of the cañon into the many fantastic forms they now present, by wearing away the softer formations, leaving the hard basalt and firmer deposits made by the hot springs standing in massive columns and spiral pinnacles of many a form and shape. The original spring-deposits, being white as snow, are stained by mineral waters of every imaginable tint, all blending delightfully together, which, when the bright sunlight pours down upon them, present an enchanting and bewildering view of forms and colors, causing the finest works of art to dwindle into insignificance when compared with the productions of Nature's Great Artificer. The process of erosion was arrested by a sudden transition from the softer material to a ledge of hard basalt, and the falls are the result.

This theory, in part at least, appears quite plausible. In our descent to the bottom of this wonderful fissure we followed part of the way the course of a little rivulet coming down from the summit, which I thought to be the sweetest water I had ever tasted, and at the bottom found a number of hot springs, while a few miles farther down the cañon they are numerous. We were told that there is, in some places, a frying, simmering sound constantly falling upon the ear, and the surroundings are much like the mouth of Tower Creek, filled with sickening odors from the mineral waters; and the water of the river is quite warm, and of a miserably alum and sulphurous taste, giving little else than vexatious disappointment to the weary and thirsty explorer who at that time and in such a place would give much for a drop of water to cool his parched tongue. On more than one occasion the tourist meets with the same disappointment, finding himself not "in a dry and thirsty land where no water is," but where a cup of pure, cold water is hard to obtain. More than once have I dashed the cup from my lips, or risen in disgust from the side of a rippling, sparkling brook where I had expected a refreshing quaff to allay my thirst, but which was tepid, tinctured with alum or sulphur, or something worse, or so hot that it would scald.

In the Grand Cañon one also will be attracted by the many-tinted colors of the mineral-stained rocks, a number of colors combining often in one small chip. The same feature is observable at other places in the basin.

Our camp was in the margin of a little park on the very verge of the cañon, and never did we sleep more sweetly than when lulled by the never-ceasing song of these two wonderful cataracts. There is much in the towering mountains, pine-forests, lovely parks, valleys, streams, and delightful cascades, surrounding the place, to add to the attractions.

Again I found myself lost in the wilderness, and as it was approaching eventide the prospect quite fair for a night with the bears and panthers (called mountain-lions in this section). Our party had gone several hours before, and had turned off the trail and camped among the pines by the river-side, while, not observing their tracks, nor the place where they had camped, I had passed on for several miles before observing the mistake, thinking I would meet them along the river in the prairie above. They fired signal-guns, but I never heard them. While on Sulphur Mountain, investigating the curious phenomena of the place, on looking down the river near the trail on which I had been traveling, I noticed the horses grazing in the valley, and returned to camp, once more relieved of the unpleasant anticipations of a lonely night in the mountains without food or shelter.

Leaving the falls, the trail follows up the bank of the river, now through a dense forest, and here and there a grassy cove, crossing frequent rills of sparkling water rippling down the mountain-sides. After a few miles we came out into a beautiful, meadow-like valley flanked with undulating hills, matted with a heavy growth of nutritious grass, which our horses enjoyed hugely, and covered with beautiful flowers glowing with the freshness of spring-time, though it was August, and interspersed with shady woodlands. Here the majestic river gives no intimation of the grand exhibition it makes below, where it attracts the wonder and admiration of the traveler from every land, but with transparent clearness and emerald tint it flows peacefully and leisurely along its channel between its low and verdant banks with slow, majestic movement, scarcely a ripple being observed upon the placid surface. It adds greatly to the loveliness of the landscape, causing one to think that everything of the grand, terrific, or diabolical, has disappeared.

From our camp at the base of the mountain we had an inviting view of the valley. While riding over this valley and its rolling foot-hills, I was forcibly reminded of the beautiful prairies of Missouri and Kansas. From the heavy growth of rich vegetation, showing the fertility of the soil, which is of good depth, it is evident that, other things equal, it would produce splendid wheat and corn. But when we remember that we are many miles from where a wagon-track was ever made, look up at those snowy mountains, there so near us, and consider that we are seven thousand feet above the level of the sea, where frost comes every month in the year, if not every night, and ice forms a half-inch thick in August (as it did in our camp last night, August 25th), all thoughts of such things suddenly vanish, and we cheerfully relinquish it to old Bruin, the numerous herds of wild game, or to the sportsman, or pleasure-seeking tourist who may come to admire its beauties and explore its adjacent wonders.

There are seemingly but two seasons in this region, winter and spring, though the former largely prevails. Even in July and August both prairie and woodland bloom with flowers of brilliant hue, possessing all the freshness of spring. They seem to follow closely the melting snows up the highest mountain side, if possible to beautify and adorn Mother Earth with a gorgeous robe, ere Winter comes again to lock everything in his icy fetters, and enshroud it with his snowy mantle. Where the trail crosses Mount Washburn we could gather snow with one hand and bouquets with the other at the same time! Some of our companions had a game at snowball, which would be rather a novel sport in August for those of our readers who live in the "sunny South," where Summer reigns perpetually.

About a mile from our camp, up the river, we cross Alum Creek—so named from the strong tincture of its sparkling waters—coming down from the divide to our right. Two or three miles farther on and ten from the falls—not far from the Yellowstone—in the midst of the prairie, is Crater Hill, or Sulphur Mountain, the Mud-Puffs and boiling springs, surrounded by remarkable formations, at which point, just after daylight, we observed numerous jets of steam ascending, which were quite interesting, and we thought we had surely arrived at Geyserland. On a beautiful morning when the sun is just rising, as the traveler, standing upon some commanding eminence, views these slender jets of steam shooting up from many clusters of springs scattered amid valleys and woodlands, and along the mountain-sides, he almost imagines that he is in a civilized land, these resembling the volumes of steam and smoke curling up from machine-shops, and flourishing hamlets, marking the abodes of industrious citizens. Instinctively you pause to hear the rumble of machinery, the shrill report of the railroad-whistle, or the thunder of the passing train. But, alas! it does not come, and the spell is soon broken by the shouts of our *buccaro*, as he brings in the animals preparatory to making our next " drive."

Visiting Sulphur Mountain, we find two oblong hills or mounds in close proximity, about one hundred and fifty feet high, one of which is flanked on the northeast side by a dense growth of pine-timber. They have been raised up in the midst of the almost level plain by thermal or volcanic agencies of some kind.

Almost the entire surface of both is perforated with numerous fissures and old craters, from which hot streams of sulphurous vapor pour forth in great abundance. We have to be careful where we sit down, and even where we walk. The fissures are lined with sulphur-crystals; and with pick and shovel great quantities of this article can be obtained just beneath the crust all over this mountain. The exterior of the mound resembles burnt clay, and the numerous steam-vents tell you of the great heat yet prevailing just below the surface.

At the western base of one of the mounds is a beautiful sulphur-spring, the basin of which is about fifteen feet in diameter, is encircled with a solid rim projecting slightly over the water of the basin, which is beautifully scalloped and corrugated with delicate bead-work of every form and shade. The water has a bright sulphur-tint, and is in a constant state of ebullition, the eruption raising almost the entire mass, throwing it from three to six feet above the surface. It literally " boils like a pot "—rather like a huge caldron. Considering its porcelain-like border so exquisitely formed and shaded, by the bright tint of the troubled water, it is quite interesting. Taking advantage of the windward side to evade the suffocating steam, from the margin of the basin we gathered a number of pebbles of various sizes, from that of a marble to a hen's-egg, which were coated with silica, some smooth, others rough like burs, which, on being broken, exhibited layers of sulphur and silica, and other minerals curiously arranged inside. Near this place is a steam-vent which acts periodically, sending up a vast volume, attended with an explosive sound. Passing over the barren, treacherous crust, not far away we found a group of real mud-caldrons from ten to fifteen feet in diameter, some containing only a mass of filthy-looking, muddy water, and others with contents about the consistency of paint and thick mortar, all at high temperature, and in a constant state of ebullition. One of them has been compared in its actions to a caldron of mush. It is far more unsightly than anything of that kind could ever appear, being of a dark, sickening cast, though of about the consistency of hasty-pudding just before it is taken from the fire. The escape of the sulphureted gas through the mud is attended with a thud-like noise, covering the surface with these puffs from which the waves recede to the shore. The ground is free from vegetation for quite a distance around. The steam-vents, and caverns, sending up the echoes from gurgling caldrons below, remind you of the importance of taking heed unto your steps. The crust in places is treacherous, and one man came near tumbling into a boiling caldron of mud, by the bank giving away; while another broke through the crust to his knees, and was severely scalded. Cold mud is bad enough, but deliver us from it when hot, and steaming with such villainous fumes! At this place we were interested in the observance of very small mounds of pyramid-form, from which issued small jets of steam, looking like perfect volcanoes in miniature.

But we leave this unsightly and unsavory place, and, after a ride of two miles across the hills to the southeast, on the bank of the river we come to another group even more unearthly in their appearance than those at Sulphur Mountain. They are much like the others, only " far more so." The contents vary in the consistency of the fluid and in the coloring, from muddy water to thick boiling mush, some tinted with sulphur-yellow, or copperas, others pink; others a bluish cast, or dark brown; and all boiling, and blubbering, and fizzing, and frying, and puffing, and looking as diabolical as anything pertaining to earth could appear. Sometimes the bubbles would rise two feet, explode with a puff, sending off their sulphurous vapor into the air, already freighted with horrible fumes. This cluster of springs covers an area of several hundred yards, and is mostly embowered in a pine-grove. The ground is broken by gulches and hills, and in our ramble we often come suddenly on an extinct crater, or on the verge of one of these boiling pits. Many of them are in close proximity, yet generally different in some phenomenal aspect.

Shortly after our arrival, guided by an immense jet of steam, attended with thunder-like reports, loud enough to be heard half a mile, we soon came to a horrible-looking pit in a grove on the slope of a hill, called the Mud Volcano. We could but think, as we looked into its steaming crater, of that passage that speaks of "an horrible pit," and were also slightly reminded of another place, where there is something said of fire and brimstone, "the smoke of which ascendeth up for ever and ever." One shrinks back with fear as he peeps into the fearful caldron, with its funnel-shaped crater, thirty feet at the top and ten or twelve at the bottom, where, at a depth of thirty feet, the dark, paint-like fluid boils and gurgles with a constant roar, which makes the earth tremble under his feet, sending up volumes of steam, which can be seen for miles, and emitting the same villainous fumes that characterize all of these horrible caldrons. The trees, for about two hundred feet on every side, are literally daubed with mud, dried on trunk and branch, which by many is thought to have been thrown from the crater when in a violent state of eruption. It is supposed by some to be a volcano, the steam having generated in a vacuum below, and, having no other means of escape, burst forth with violent explosion, hurling earth and trees and boiling mud in every direction. The freshness of the mud indicates that, if a volcano, it is either of recent origin, having thrown up the mud when it first broke out, or, having been in action for years, is choked up at times by the caving-in of the sides, causing it to relieve itself by hurling the muddy contents many feet into the air. Both theories are possible. However, it gave no signs of eruption while we were there. It had the appearance of the channel of a dark, turbid river rolling along below the surface, as we could, now and then, when the dense cloud of steam passed away, see through the orifice. The loud report from the escaping steam, and the hollow gurgling of the liquid contents, seemed to indicate the country to which it belonged, and echo upward to earth in doleful tones the fate of him who should fall into its infernal depths. But some have recently claimed that it is no volcano at all, and that the mud with which the surrounding pines are draped is formed from the constantly-rising vapor, which is freighted with this same composition. This is quite plausible, and I am inclined to think it the correct theory.

Not far from here, just down the hill, there is a vast cavern, the sides and entrance of which are covered with a soft, greenish sediment, deposited from mineral-charged gases, on which many curious travelers have inscribed their names. The roof, though at the mouth sufficiently elevated to admit a man of full stature, slopes gradually backward to the water's edge. Though we confess a good share of curiosity, we forbear to enter here, being met by huge bursting bubbles of water dashing against the roof of the cavern, emitting forcible volumes of sulphurous steam, soon driving us from the place. This is known as Giant's Caldron, which we leave in utter disgust, and, following up the river a short distance, right by the trail leading to the lake, we come to Muddy Geyser, the first spring of geyser-like pretensions that we have seen yet, and a poor specimen it is. Here is a basin of dark, muddy, lead-colored water, about a hundred feet in diameter, and which you would never suspect of being a geyser should you pass when it is not in action, but would pass it by as any other pool of filthy-looking, muddy water, just as we did, until attracted thither by the rush of escaping steam and the roar of surging billows. It flows at regular intervals of about six hours, and continues in action fifteen minutes, throwing up a vast volume of the muddy fluid, ten or fifteen feet in diameter, to an average height of fifteen feet, while an occasional jet reaches the extraordinary altitude of thirty or forty feet. Guided hither by the strange report, we found the water in the hitherto-sleeping basin surging to and fro at a wonderful rate. At times it seemed that almost the entire mass in the basin would be raised to a height of several feet, which would be pierced and broken by rising columns of steam, throwing it in every direction, after which it would be quiet for a moment, though only to repeat the operation, which is continued until the flow is ended. The orifice is shaped like a funnel, the sides lined principally with clay. The eruption is caused by the escape of steam generated below the surface, sending out the usual diabolical odors. But little water escapes from the basin during the flow, and, after the action, it nearly all sinks into the funnel, and is quite tranquil, gradually rising until time for another eruption.

Camping here two nights on our return, we had a good opportunity to watch its movements, with that of the other springs. But the revolting and unearthly appearance of these mud-caldrons, together with the foulness of the odors they send forth; the anything but wholesome contents; the noisy ebullition; and the general appearance of desolation that surrounds all such places, soon satisfied our curiosity, and, though filled with wonder at what our eyes have seen, we pass on without much desire to turn. We wonder that the diabolical vocabulary was not again drawn upon in naming these unsavory places, but suppose it was exhausted before the explorer discovered this region, or that things began to appear too real to be trifled with in any such manner.

CHAPTER X.

Alum Creek.—Interesting Group of Hot Springs.—The "Flutter-Wheel."—Our Guide.—Mary's Lake.—Lower Geyser Basin.—Thud-Geyser.—The Fountain.—"Young Hopeful."—Journey up the River.—Vexations of the Way.—Tumble in the Mud.—Captain C——'s Misfortune.—Boiling Lakes.—Arrival at Upper Basin.—Wonderful Change.

WE returned to our camp on the Yellowstone, where the cook had prepared our noonday lunch, to which we did ample justice. The *buccaro* drove in the horses, which were saddled and packed, when we commenced our line of march westward up Alum Creek, which comes down from the divide between the Madison and Yellowstone Rivers. Our journey was over a rolling, prairie country, carpeted mostly with a mat of luxuriant vegetation. The view of the mountains, mantled with forests of pine that come down to the borders of the lovely park, which is dotted here and there with groves of timber, gave us a fine landscape-view; while the refreshing noonday breeze, just down from the regions of snow, made it a delightful ride. We camped in a little cove, surrounded by towering pines, near the source of the stream.

Not far from our camp is quite an interesting group of hot springs, the water containing various minerals, but carrying chiefly a strong solution of iron, which shows itself in the deposit everywhere on the mountain-side. The crust around the springs is hard and rusty-looking, like iron, and the deposit assumes almost every conceivable form. The water, simmering and gurgling and boiling up in a dozen or more different caldrons, often splashing up from its pot-like basins several feet in the air, reminds you of an extensive group of furnaces. Quite a stream of water flows along the channel of the little creek, which is almost at boiling heat. My attention was arrested by an unusual, fluttering kind of sound, which was caused by the forcible discharge of a small volume of hot water from a fissure right in the bed of the creek, and which comes through and above the surface of the main channel, giving off a vibrating noise, much like that of a flutter-wheel. So different from the rest, it appears quite comic and curious, and will attract the attention of the passer-by.

Next day—August 29th—we were to arrive at the real Geyserland. So we were up at an early hour, cooked and ate breakfast, preparatory to an early start, while John Werk, our horseman and guide, went after the stock.

John is the conductor of our party through the park. He is a thick-set, sandy-whiskered, and usually (when all works well) a good-natured fellow, and a perfect type of an old-time mountaineer. Clad in buckskin, fringed and ornamented in the usual style, mounted on his pony, and armed with blacksnake and spurs, and at the head of a pack-train or party of tourists, he is in the zenith of his glory. He knows the camping-places and curiosities of this region, and, if possible, takes his passengers through on time. But, like other mortals, he loses his patience sometimes, and he brings in his ponies with—
"Plague their pesky hides; they'll pay for this tantrum!" coming from his lips, and emphasized by even stronger expressions, which indicate that something has gone wrong.

"Sinch your saddles tight, and see that the packs are on good," he remarks, as we are getting ready, "for we go through timber as thick as the hair on a dog's back, and down the longest, steepest mountain on the road. We'll have to go through a swamp that'll mire a muskeeter; and, if we're out after night, it'll be darker than the thickets in Egypt."

Everything in readiness, we moved out, continuing our westerly course, passing numerous mounds and sulphur-springs, some of them sending off a rumbling sound, and loading the atmosphere with their disgusting odors. We passed along the bank of a lovely little lakelet, sleeping in seclusion in the shade of towering evergreens, by which it is sheltered from the roaring tempests. It is near the divide, and on its pebbly shore some members of our party unfurled the Stars and Stripes, and christened it Mary's Lake, in honor of Miss Clark, a young lady belonging to our party. Descending the mountain, and following the tortuous windings of the trail, leading through an almost impenetrable forest, we are soon on a tributary of the Madison, which we follow for several miles, partly through an open country, when, turning our course southward for a short distance through a neck of timber, we suddenly find ourselves in the Lower Geyser Basin, situated on the Firehole River, the principal branch of the Madison. Here, along the river, is an open space of one or more square miles, in the dense forest enshrouding the neighboring hills, containing hundreds of hot springs, surrounded by all manner of fantastic formations; lakes of hot water, real geysers, and other curiosities, which are the result of subterranean heat seeking an outlet through the various openings in the siliceous deposit. At any other place they would be marvels to the curious traveler; but, being so near the grand geysers of the world, where the wonder-seeking tourist's enthusiasm generally reaches its climax, they lose much of the attraction they would otherwise possess.

The springs are much more numerous here than in the upper basin, but do not assume such geyser-like pretensions. A few of them, however, though inferior in grandeur and extent, are of sufficient importance to be classed with their more highly-favored neighbors, throwing the water at times in considerable quantities to the height of fifty feet, and making no little display in the effort.

The action of the Thud-Geyser is attended with a detonation similar to the firing of a cannon underground. The Fountain is said to be quite captivating when in action, and the name is suggestive of its general appearance.

We camped in the basin, but visited only one cluster of springs, where we were highly entertained, however, for a short time, by the comic manœuvres of a small spring, which, seemingly taking advantage of our ignorance, would fain make us believe it belonged to the wonders we had come so far to behold. There was a moderate-sized, funnel-like basin, with a small aperture at the bottom, through which the water and steam find an outlet. The water quietly but steadily rises in the funnel, when, all at once, without any warning, it begins to boil, and bubble, and spurt, and splash about, at a fearful rate, sometimes raising the whole mass a foot or more, when a little jet will spout up through it to a height of ten feet, and all the time fussing and spitting out its boiling contents in a spiteful, saucy manner. Some one filled the crater with pebbles, and it was amusing to see it throw them out. A wag christened it "Young Hopeful"—a suggestive title. It acts every few hours, and doubtless has geyser-like aspirations. After amusing ourselves for a time watching the movements of these springs, we returned to our camp in the verge of the woodland, and were soon seeking rest in slumber, for which the events of the day had given us a relish.

Next day we continued our journey southward up the Firehole River (only the Madison, with another name), which rises in the Madison Lake, south and a little west of here, near the main range of the Rocky Mountains. The trail—where there is one—follows a tortuous, serpentine course, through the thickest timber we ever saw, which was filled in with fire-slashes of fallen trees, making a complicated network, and presenting an almost insurmountable barrier, which is by no means agreeable to the pleasure-seeking equestrian; and last, though not least, leading through next to fathomless swamps of the filthiest water and the blackest and muddiest mud—as the ladies in the party, who had a good opportunity to test it, will testify—to be found in the world. This increases the numerous other vexations of a trip through a wild mountain-country, and, if possible, exhausts the last vestige of the little stock of patience one has succeeded in bringing thus far on the journey. You have need to be sparing of this precious article, for you will require all that you are able to muster before you complete the grand rounds on horseback, especially if you are unfortunate in selecting your riding-horse, and are not an expert rider. Just imagine, if you will, a man on a moderate-sized *cayuse*, navigating one of these old-fashioned swamps, such as they have in the Missouri and Mississippi bottoms, where the ground shakes for twenty feet around, threatening every moment, but for the intervening trees and rubbish, to ingulf both horse and rider, causing serious misgivings of his ever being able to reach the shore! Then, at the same time, climbing over a fallen trunk, making a short angle to avoid some barrier in front, and twisting and dodging, and turning the body in every conceivable shape to avoid collision with contiguous logs and trees; keeping yourself free from the grasp of overhanging limbs, which threaten you with, if possible, a worse than Absalom's fate, together with efforts to maintain your equilibrium in the saddle—and all this taking place at the *same moment*, or as nearly so as can be imagined! The man may consider himself fortunate who maintains his position in the saddle, and goes through dry-shod; and the lady may be grateful who keeps free from the fallen timber, and escapes without a tumble in the mud: for more than one gentleman and lady of lofty aspirations and aristocratic pretensions have suddenly been wounded in spirit by being unhorsed in such a miserable place. The young lady along with our party did not escape a promiscuous tumble in the mud, though receiving no injury from it, and greatly enjoyed the fun after she had regained the saddle. Not so with our aristocratic friend Captain C——, who, by the sudden and unexpected stopping of his horse just when it was highly important that he should go forward, was precipitated head-foremost over the animal's head, and sent sprawling to the earth, which was all but solid, and found himself unwillingly trying the depth of the mud and water, retaining enough on his person to remind his comrades of the catastrophe, to the utter discomfiture of our tasty comrade, whose pride suffered more than his person. But do not imagine that it is so difficult all the way up, and let not the danger of the journey keep you away.

Here and there, along the river-bank on both sides, are numerous groups of caldrons and boiling springs. About three miles from the Lower Basin, on the west side of the Firehole, are three of the most remarkable of these thermal springs. Two of them are on slight elevations or mounds, and are almost real lakes (they are so large) of boiling water, the basins being several hundred feet in diameter, with borders beautifully ornamented—the very hot water, with its ultramarine shade, so transparent as to reveal the beautiful, moss-like, silky lining, covering the sides of the basin to fabulous depths. One, on the side of the slope, not far from the river, is altogether unlike the others, and creates quite a different sensation. It has apparently broken out near the river-bank, and enlarged itself by the caving in of the sides, extending back several hundred feet; the softer formation underneath wearing away by the constant action of the water, and leaving the harder substance of the crust extending over the rim of the basin. The dark-colored, treacherous, and gloomy-looking walls rise from twenty to thirty feet above the water on three sides. The constant agitation of the water, boiling up for three or four feet above the surface, sending up an angry, rumbling sound; the dense volumes of continuously-rising steam, freighted with offensive sulphurous fumes, which it emits; together with the dark and dismal overhanging walls, bring a feeling of horror over the beholder as he gazes into the seething pit. We instinctively step back, lest by a too near approach and a crumble of the unsafe and treacherous wall we should drop into the steaming lake, where we would be beyond the reach of human help. One is vividly reminded of the scenes in Dante's "Inferno." Could we but have heard the cries of the tormented, Bunyan's picture of the pit in the side of the hill which the pilgrims were shown by the shepherds on their way to the Celestial City, where they "looked in and saw that it was very dark and smoky;" thought that they "heard a rumbling noise as of fire, and a cry of some tormented, and that they smelt the fumes of brimstone," would have been complete.

"That looks like the burning lake itself," says one.

"If this ain't about as close to it as a man can go with a pack-horse, then I don't want a cent," remarks a waggish fellow, standing near.

"Faith, and ye might be afther gettin' a leetle nearer on foot sometimes, Billy, if ye ain't careful, me boy," responds a son of Erin, who is making the grand rounds.

After continuing our ride six miles farther up the river

southward over the trail partly described above, some of our party choosing the channel of the river with its solid bottom, in preference to the treacherous swamps and fallen timber, for a portion of the way, without any further accident or mishap worthy of notice, at twelve o'clock A. M., August 30th, we arrived in the Upper Geyser Basin of Firehole River, which is the centre of attraction in the National Park, and the grand geyser-region of the world, and where in future years, not far hence, either, the philosophers and tourists, and the lovers of the sublime and the wonderful in Nature, will gather from all countries and climes to make investigation, to behold and wonder, and even worship at Nature's shrine. How sudden the transition! How delightful and soul-inspiring the effect! But yesterday we were admiring the beauty of charming landscapes, emerald-tinted, peaceful lakelets, and murmuring, sparkling streamlets, or charmed at the wonderful displays of Nature's beauties and curiosities in the Lower Basin; and but two hours ago we were admiring the beauties of a lovely river, winding through a gloomy solitude; gazing with horror into a seething caldron, or urging our jaded cayuses amid the perils of a desolate, marshy wilderness; but now, suddenly, the journey is ended, and we are ushered into a land of marvelous wonders and mysterious, soul-entrancing, indescribable beauties, where everything is life and animation ; and the beholder is soon lost to the dangers and vexations of the way, rapt in delightful bewilderment, and carried away with the enchantments of this mystic region. One imagines that he is no longer in the same country, and that, on his upward march toward the "crest of the world," he has arrived in some fairy city of dazzling beauty and splendor. The first impulse, after the spell is broken, and you find that this region is really on our own Mother Earth, is to throw your hat into the air, and shout aloud for joy.

CHAPTER XI.

Upper Geyser Basin.—Meeting with Friends.—Our Camp "Doing" the Geysers.—"Old Faithful."—The Sentinel.—First Eruption witnessed.—Description.—The Crater.—Ornamentation of the Mound.—Beehive.—Giantess.—Fearful-looking Cavity.—Langford's Description.—Refusal to accommodate Less Distinguished Personages.—Castle Geyser.—Beautiful Mound-Spring.

LEST the reader should consider me extravagant, and accuse me of forgetting that he is yet ignorant of the mystic charms of this land of enchantment, I must introduce him to some of the surroundings. But never did language seem more inadequate to the task, nor my efforts at pen-picturing so sadly felt, as I attempt a portrayal of the utterly indescribable wonders of the Upper Geyser Basin. I am tempted to throw away the pen in disgust.

Here, also, is an opening in the surrounding forest, doubtless caused by volcanic agencies or powerful thermal activities, as the numerous trunks and branches of trees imbedded in the siliceous deposit around the geysers and springs, and in the calcareous sediment all over the basin, will testify. The opening containing the principal geysers extends about a mile up and down the river, and from a quarter to a half mile across, interspersed here and there with scattered trees and groves of pine. We camped in one of these little groves, where we found protection from the burning rays of the sun, and could enjoy the refreshing breeze; and, being in a convenient locality near the centre of the basin, we had a splendid view of the principal objects of interest. The horses were sent out to a grassy park a mile up the river, to feast upon the nutritious bunch-grass; and as wood was convenient, and hot and cold water in abundance, we were prepared to "do" the wonders of Wonderland at our leisure.

The basin is covered mostly with a whitish crust of geyserite, or siliceous deposit, which is usually hard enough even to bear a horse. Here and there, however, is a treacherous, boggy swamp which we do well to avoid. The geysers and principal springs are surrounded with deposits of the various minerals formed into cones, pyramids, castles, and grottoes, of every conceivable design. The surface is perforated with steam-vents from a half inch to five feet in diameter. Just imagine the steam coming up from a thousand orifices, the transparent element spouting forth from a dozen caldrons at once; and the whole scene, beautiful and strange within itself, bathed with the bright sunlight pouring down from a cloudless sky, softening and blending the variegated hues of the groundwork, and arching every column of steam with a halo of brilliant colors! Is it not enough to bewilder and overwhelm the curiosity-seeking tourist and lover of the wonderful?

Here we met with a number of kind friends, who had preceded us but a few hours; and, after taking a hasty lunch, we sallied forth to feast our curiosity, and explore the wonders of Geyserland, with a satisfaction that is better felt than told. We invite the reader to go with us, as we are a cheerful and congenial group, and expect a good time.

We will first visit the Old Faithful, so called from the regular intervals at which she spouts. She stands as a sentinel on that eminence yonder at the head of the basin, near the timber on the west side of the river, about a quarter of a mile southeast of our camp; and, though on the outpost of this mystic region, she never flinches from duty, nor asks relief, but by the hourly rush of steam, and the grand display of water-works, she sounds the "All's well!" reminding the inhabitants that she is at her post, and that the machinery of the lower region is yet in working condition. It is nearly time for her to spout, and we must be in haste if we would witness the first eruption at close range. Here we found several mounds, perhaps the craters of extinct geysers; but the crater of the Faithful is on an elevation made by the deposit from the water about twenty or thirty feet above the common level, with a chimney-like crater rising five or six feet higher. Full of adventure, we walked up to the steaming aperture, but warned by the internal rumbling and quaking of the ground beneath us, attended by a rush of steam and water from the crater, we beat a hasty retreat, and had scarcely reached a place of safety, when, turning our eyes, we beheld one of the grandest displays of the kind we had ever beheld—a perfect geyser—an immense volume of clear, hot water projected into the air one hundred and twenty-five or one hundred and fifty vertical feet, attended with dense volumes of steam rising upward for many hundred feet, and floating away in clouds. So great was the impellent force, that the immense fountain was held in its place for several moments, only swayed to and fro by the gentle breeze, the water descending on all sides, and rushing down the slopes of the mound in great channels. Every spectator was filled with enthusiasm at this the first exhibition of the kind we had yet witnessed. The crater is oblong in shape, being two feet wide by six in length, which gives you an estimate of the dimension of the volume of water thrown out, the average height of which is about one hundred and twenty-five feet. The immense volume impelled from the crater forms a perfect apex at the top, where the water having spent its force descends on the outside of the ascending column, giving it, when the wind is favorable, driving away the steam, the appearance of a cone, nearly the shape of a sugar-loaf. The sparkling fountain lashed into foam, detached into millions of pearly drops, and all glistening in the bright sunlight, is grand beyond conception, and creates an enthusiasm that is perfectly irresistible. The water often at first goes up in jets or by successive impulses, as if the firemen were letting the steam on by degrees, each jet going higher, and still higher, when, after it has maintained its greatest altitude for a few moments, it descends in the same way until the force is spent. The last minute or so the eruption is entirely of steam. When it becomes quiescent (and slightly cools) we can approach the orifice, and look down into the throat for many feet, but can only hear the water angrily boiling and slowly preparing for another display.

The deposit around the crater is somewhat peculiar, being of a hard, stony character, mostly silica, with a metallic grayish cast. Sloping gently from the orifice, the surface of the mound on every side is full of cavities, descending in successive terraces, which are covered with little urns or basins arranged into every conceivable form, divided by curious and delicately-wrought partitions, much like those at the Mammoth Springs, and constantly full of beautifully clear water. The edges of many of these basins, as also the throat of the geyser, are covered with silica, and corrugated and ornamented with a delicate coral-like formation, like beads and pearls of a beautiful porcelain, and yellowish or saffron hue. In some of the little urns are delicate columns or stems surmounted with small tablets or caps just at the surface of the water, reminding one of toadstools, cauliflowers, or flowers growing in the water. In others there are oval-shaped pebbles, and stalagmites and coral-like forms of every texture and tint. Growing up amid a cloud of water and spray surcharged with the materials which are wrought into so many shapes, the colors are kept bright, and the work appears as delicately as a butterfly's plumage, but is so hard that you require an axe or some heavy instrument to secure a specimen. In the midst of such wonders we are again wafted to the abode of the fairies, and can but think of the wonderful story of Aladdin and his lamp, and a dozen similar ones, so bewitching are the beauties of this region. The water in the pools is so transparent that, doubting our eyes, we could but sound its depth with a stick, or by inserting our hands. As you recede from the summit, where the water grows cooler in its downward flow, the basins are larger, and the texture of the stony deposit proportionately coarse. Imbedded in this mound we notice the remains of several trees which are silicified, some of them furnishing beautiful specimens for a cabinet.

We have lingered here longer than we intended, but have done so because this is the first geyser visited, and this account is an answer to many questions that we have been asked frequently since our visit there, and also describes the general features of nearly all of these wonderful curiosities. They are all different, however, in some peculiar feature, owing to the temperature of the water, and the shape and size of the geyser-tube.

But, leaving the Faithful, and crossing the river on a fallen tree, gathering a sprig and cone from an evergreen as we pass, as a memento of our visit, about three hundred yards distant down the stream, and not far from its margin, on the side of the slope, we come to a little cone of the same siliceous character, with perfect symmetry of form, and beautifully corrugated with pearl-like bead-work. It is three feet in height, nearly circular in form, and from three to four feet in diameter at the top, with a base of eight feet. Its aperture is about eighteen inches in diameter, and ornamented in its peculiar geyser-like style. This is the Beehive Geyser, so called from its appearance —that of a beehive. Standing alone on the hill-side, you would not at first suspect that it belonged to the geyser family, as there is but little evidence of the action of water around it. But while we were in camp the next day after our arrival, some one shouted: "Geyser! geyser! the Beehive! the Beehive's going off!" when we looked, and beheld a stream of water and steam, somewhat larger than the aperture, ascending gracefully and without any apparent effort from this small orifice, until it reached an altitude of at least two hundred feet. It makes a fine display as the water and steam come up in a steady stream (unlike most of the others), and continues in action about fifteen minutes. We were captivated at the sight, and in the midst of our excitement waded the river in order to have the full benefit of a closer view. We could stand within a few feet of the base on the windward side, while the water and steam were hurled with great force into the air. This geyser acts only once in every two or three days, and, being one of great beauty, is a general favorite

On the same side of the river, about two hundred yards to the eastward from the Beehive, on the summit of a little knoll, is the Giantess, which, according to the evidence of some of the first explorers, is one of the grandest and most magnificent geysers in the basin when in action. Here is an orifice, with edges beautifully scalloped, about twenty by twenty-five feet in diameter at the surface, and filled to the brim with water, which is at about 192° temperature, and very slightly troubled. No one would suspect its being a geyser, but simply a mineral spring, such as crown some other eminences near here, were it not for the great channels and water-marks made by the descending torrent as it rushes down the hill-side, after

"THE GIANTESS."

being released from the heated chambers far down in the bowels of the earth. But how different the scene two hours later, when attracted by repeated sounds like claps of thunder, and heavy concussions like the firing of a cannon underground, and about as regular as the discharges of a battery in a siege, causing the earth to tremble beneath our feet, and filling one with horror that would cause many to fear and tremble, and hearing the rumble and rush of falling water, accompanied by the hiss of powerful steam-valves in motion, we hastened to the scene of action, which proved to be the Giantess! She was just getting up, or rather it proved to be letting off, steam; and from the internal rumble of her machinery we anticipated a fine display. We found this great orifice nearly sixty-five feet in depth, half emptied, and the water foaming and heaving and surging at a terrible rate, throwing occasional volumes (a few scores of barrels each) out of the crater to the height of fifty feet, which came down with a fearful crash. At times the water would recede entirely from view, and we could look down into the terrible cavity, made more gloomy by the grim, dark walls, to its greatest depth. But more than once were we driven from the verge by the rising steam, as if, spiteful at our intrusion, it would cast out the boiling volumes and threaten us with destruction. This action was repeated occasionally for several hours, until after dark; but it positively refused to give us one of its grandest displays, of which a writer before quoted says: "When an eruption is about to occur, the basin gradually fills with boiling water to within a few feet of the surface, when suddenly with heavy concussions immense clouds of steam rise to the height of five hundred feet, and the whole great body of water—twenty by twenty-five feet —ascends in one gigantic column to the height of ninety feet. From the apex of this column five great jets shoot up, radiating slightly from each other, to the unparalleled altitude of two hundred and fifty feet. The earth trembles under the descending deluge from this vast fountain; a thousand hissing sounds are heard in the air; rainbows encircle the summits of the jets with a halo of celestial glory. The falling water ploughs up and bears away the shelly strata, and a seething flood pours down the slope and into the river. After playing thus for twenty minutes, it gradually subsides; the water lowers into the crater out of sight; the steam ceases to escape, and all is quiet." It played several times for Dr. Hayden's party, but for less distinguished personages it seems to have a contempt, as but few have ever seen it as above described. I think, however, its glory is departing.

Near here are a number of springs and caldrons, with remarkable formations, crowning the little knolls on which they are located, and some of them boiling and spouting away with geyser-like pretensions.

Recrossing the Firehole River to the west side, passing our camp on the way, and following down the stream a short distance, about four hundred yards from the Giantess, just at the border of a little grove, we come to a remarkable formation resembling in a striking manner the ruins of some ancient fortress. It will attract your attention as soon as you enter the basin, and has been styled the "Castle Geyser"—a very appropriate title. The mound is several feet above the common surface, and is crowned with a chimney-shaped crater of ten feet in height, and perhaps eight feet in diameter. The formation is siliceous, and contains numerous branches of trees, and even trunks incrusted with the grayish deposit. We ascend by steps or terraces, which are quite regular; and about the orifice, which is three feet in diameter, we find large globular masses of an orange-color, figured with the usual sponge-like corals.

MUD SPRINGS.

The water in the crater is constantly troubled, boiling and fretting, sending up steam and occasional jets of water to a height of twenty or thirty feet. It was in its day, perhaps, one of the grandest of the groups, and even yet at intervals makes displays that may well put others to the blush, sending up an immense body of water to an altitude of fifty feet, which is attended with heavy concussions and internal rumblings, and continues in steady action for one or two hours. It did not act while we were in the basin, though I have been told by those who have seen it that the effect is very fine; and so desirous were some of our party of seeing it that they arose at midnight. But it proved to be a "false alarm."

A few steps from the crater of the Castle, and on the same mound, is one of those famous central springs, such as crown the summit of many a little mound both in the basin and scattered through the woods, whose beauties mortal eyes have never been permitted to admire. This is one of the most lovely and exquisitely beautiful springs in all Wonderland. For beauty of coloring and delicacy of arrangement it cannot be surpassed. It is about ten feet in diameter. Its scalloped border of the finest texture, and embracing in its arrangement all that is beautiful; the projecting rim, and the delicately-colored sides as seen in the emerald-tinted depths of the marvelously transparent water, present a scene that never is forgotten, and which beggars description. This spring is not boisterous like others, and does not seem to overflow, though the temperature is just sufficient to keep it slightly troubled upon the surface, which, as it vibrates under the bright rays of the noonday sun, brings into play all the prismatic colors which, blending with the countless hues of the decorations on the sides of the basin, and observed in the ultramarine depths before us, presents a scene so perfectly fascinating to the lover of the beautiful, that he again forgets his surroundings, and is wafted away from this mundane sphere to the "land of joy and beauty," and all the brilliant scenes of fairy regions seem to be fully realized. In the fiery depths he can picture bowers, and coves, and chambers, all fantastically arranged and embroidered, which one might believe to be the outskirts of Fairyland itself; and he is tempted to look for some good genius to appear and unlock the mysterious gate that ushers him into the delightful realm, with its wonderful temples, its golden thrones, marble palaces, Elysian fields, silvery fountains, and mysterious inhabitants, where he can revel amid the glories of that unknown land. We found our friend Colonel Sanders standing by this spring gazing intently into its depths, and perfectly fascinated with its beauty.

CHAPTER XII.

Curiosity.—New Mode of Washing.—Cooking in a Geyser.—Disappointed Expectations—Dish-Washing.—Bridget takes Revenge.—" Taken in."—Grand Geyser.—Turban.—The Saw-Mill, *alias* "Rustler."—Old Chimneys.—Extinct Geysers.—Amusing Incident.—" Attack in the Rear."—" Change of Base."—River-side.—Comet.—Fantail Geyser.—The Grotto.—Quaint Formation.—The Giant Geyser, the Grandest in the World.—Wonderful Eruption.—Two Hundred and Fifty Feet in the Air.—Intense Excitement.

What curiosity-loving mortals we are! Always seeking something new. And the geysers afford opportunity for more than one inventive genius to try some unknown and hitherto unthought of experiment. "Can we not avoid the labor of laundry-work?" says one; and immediately commits his task to Old Faithful, with orders to return his washing faithfully in one hour. But making no pretensions to faithfulness, only in her line of business—*spouting*—many articles that go into her chambers "ne'er come out again;" though what she does return is in the finest order. We were out but one 'kerchief, which we supposed was kept to pay the bill. One gentleman tried boiling his dinner in a geyser-spring, but a sudden eruption foiled his plans, blasted his hopes, leaving him dinnerless and disgusted with the business. We heard of another curiosity-loving, labor-saving philosopher, who was discharging the honors of the culinary department, and, having a natural abhorrence of dish-washing, in his musings he fell upon a plan, and, enthusiastic at his new discovery, enticed by the bubbling of the water in a lovely-looking little basin near by, he hastened to give them over to his new servant, and, reposing all confidence in his newly-found Bridget, he was lost again in meditation upon the advantages of a life in Geyserland, when, all at once, his ears were greeted with an unusual rustling, splashing report. He looked out, and, behold! the hitherto quiet little spring, as if indignant at the insult offered, was writhing and spouting and splashing about at a fearful rate, and tossing knives and forks, spoons, plates, and cups, around in utter disgust. No time was to be lost, and, with disappointed expectations and scalded fingers, the dishes were rescued from the perilous situation, and were more fortunate than the philosopher, who was evidently "taken in" for one time.

But leaving the Castle and its fascinating spring, following a circuitous route to evade the boggy places in the ravines, we found a foot-log, on which we recrossed the river to the east side; and, about one-eighth of a mile from the Castle, situated at the base of a small elevation near the edge of the timber, we found the famous Grand Geyser. Unlike the majority of the others, it has no raised cone, but only a funnel-shaped basin, which sinks below the level. The basin is some forty feet in diameter, in the centre of which is the orifice or mouth of the geyser-tube, about two and a half by four feet. In connection with this basin, though slightly elevated above it, is another, with a quadrangular-shaped rim, about twelve by twenty-five feet from border to border, in the centre of which is an orifice of three or four feet in diameter. This basin is three feet above the other; is most of the time full of water, which is generally quite turbulent, boiling up several feet above the surface, and constantly emptying its contents into the basin of the Grand, which is very quiet when not spouting.

It is impossible to portray the beauty of the fantastically-shaped siliceous formations with which the rims, basins, etc., of these two springs are decorated; the rounded, spongiform, coral-figured masses, of every conceivable appearance, often resembling turbans, some one even comparing them to squashes or pumpkins, which resemblance is increased by their yellowish hue; then the hundreds of little reservoirs and shallow basins, arranged with a charming irregularity, scalloped, pearly, bead-like borders, separated by elegantly-formed partitions, with every variety of coloring from the different minerals in the water, showing the handiwork of a Master-Artist, and, though so delicate in appearance, so solid that a hatchet is often necessary to obtain a choice piece for your cabinet. As remarked before, the general feature of the deposit around these craters is much the same, though each one has its characteristic arrangement and ornamentation. Sometimes silica prevails, sometimes alumina; at others the whole is shaded and strongly tinctured with sulphur or iron. It is marvelous to see the thousand forms and types of beauty presented; though diversified, each system is perfect in itself. These two springs are contiguous, but have no connection underneath, and the action of one does not affect the other. One would think the noisy, sputtering spring—called the Turban—was the spouter, and would never imagine that the quiet, unpretentious basin just below is one of the grandest fountains of the Upper Basin. But such is the case. It throws a stream of water, the size of the aperture, to a height of two hundred feet, accompanied by immense clouds of steam, the wonderful volume of water descending in the basin, together with the internal detonations shaking the very earth beneath to a great distance. It spouts at intervals of about twenty-four hours, and continues in action for fifteen or twenty minutes. The grandeur of its appearance when making one of its finest displays on a bright, sunshiny day caused the explorers to give it the name of Grand Geyser. At daylight on the morning after our arrival I was aroused from a refreshing slumber by fearful subterranean reports, as regular as pulse-beats, just as though an enormous hammer was being hurled with wonderful force against the very foundation of the earth right beneath us, and, guided by the noise, I arrived here just in time to see this geyser in action. The basin was nearly full of water, agitated by the escape of dense masses of steam, when, all at once, with another report, as if from the engineer below giving the signal to commence, and with but little effort, a column of water gracefully rose to the height of nearly one hundred and fifty feet, and was kept in position at that altitude for several minutes, the descending masses flowing away in a large stream, and the immense volumes of steam lingering around, mantling the beautiful fountain, and depriving us of a good view. The column at first, however, rose above the steam, and, after its force was exhausted, retired within the funnel out of sight. It was not one of her grandest efforts, but sufficient to give the spectator some idea of its glory.

One hundred yards from the Grand, toward the river, on the hill-side, is the Saw-Mill Geyser, which, from its industry, being in action about half the time, and the comical character of its manœuvres, will not fail to bring itself into notice, though right in the shadow of the Grand. The orifice is only six inches, surrounded by a shallow basin, having a radius of ten feet. The basin is covered with pebbles and bits of silicified pine, which are beautifully ornamented by the showers of mineral-freighted water almost constantly falling upon them. When in action, the basin is full to the brim and running over, and the steam, puffing up from the aperture in small quantities, making a noise much like the escape of steam from the pipe of a saw-mill, suggested the name. It raises a great body of water

IN THE GEYSER BASIN.

several feet, when, just as it is falling back, with a spasmodic and unusual effort, it is met by successive columns of steam, and quickly hurled upward again twenty-five feet into the air, with an occasional jet reaching the altitude of forty feet, when it is detached, and descends in crystal showers, producing, in the sunlight, a fine effect. It is interesting and quite exciting, especially in the absence of more magnificent wonders. We were highly entertained by watching its movements for nearly an hour, casting in pebbles to see them tossed out in every direction. Not knowing at the time its name, I dubbed it "The Rustler" (a word much used in the mountains, indicative of energy and activity), which my traveling-companions thought quite expressive, though a lady friend, perhaps with finer taste, named it "The Fountain." Surely it deserves a better title than the one it has.

Near this point, along the river-bank, are a number of chimney-like craters, which Dr. Hayden thinks are the remains of extinct geysers. They are full of water, in some of which it is at a high temperature, though not sufficient to produce eruptions. There are many such craters and springs all through Wonderland, which may have once been active geysers, but are now extinct; while others, though still active, erupt only at long intervals, and have not been discovered yet. It is sometimes difficult to distinguish between geysers and inactive springs when the former are not spouting, except by the channels in the shelly strata showing traces of the descending fountain as it flows away.

While near the Saw-mill, on our first round, a little incident occurred which is too good to be lost. The surface at this point is perforated with numerous apertures and fissures, some of which, though too small to be readily observed, furnish vents for heated air from the regions below. Before going to the lower part of the basin we had stopped for a few moments, hoping to witness an eruption from the Castle, and, to pass the time agreeably, one of the party was relating an anecdote, to which the rest were listening attentively. One of our friends had thrown himself on the ground carelessly, in the shade of a small pine, his face wearing the very expression of satisfaction and delight, when, all at once, as if stung by a hornet, with fearfully-distorted features and violent gesticulations, his hands forcibly striking toward the seat of his trousers, he hastily came to his feet, and, as soon as breath would permit, exclaimed with vehemence: "Geyser! geyser! I'm sitting on a geyser!" It was evidently an "attack in the rear," causing a "change of base" in double-quick. He had sat down on a steam-vent. We all laughed heartily at the joke, and continued our rambles.

Following down the river on the same (east) side, and passing numerous cones and hot and cold springs, we came to the River-side Geyser, with an oddly-formed crater, on the river-bank, in action almost constantly, but of moderate pretensions as to the height of its column. Not far from this is the prettily fashioned crater of the Fan, so called from the appearance of its fountain when in action. It is at the lower extremity of the Upper Basin, where we must change our course. The Fan, or Fantail Geyser, is said to be one of the prettiest spouters in this region. Its machinery is surely the most complicated of any, and, having five distinct orifices, it sends up as many jets of water and steam, sometimes reaching an altitude of a hundred feet, the jets ascending and descending in such a manner as to resemble the outlines of a feather fan. It spreads itself three or four times a day, and is greatly admired by all who witness it, some of the spectators growing wild with enthusiasm at the gorgeous display.

Recrossing the river once more, and following up the west

THE "GIANT" GEYSER.

bank a short distance, about one hundred yards from the stream, we come to a cluster of springs, at one side of which, on a bed of white silica, stands a mound of grotesque appearance, about twenty feet above the surrounding level. This is the crater of Grotto Geyser, noted principally for the curious, complicated, and irregularly-shaped walls surrounding the orifice, and the beautifully-wrought ornamentation with which they are surmounted. Here Nature has again shown her handiwork in the striking ingenuity of the arrangement and coloring of this quaint formation. It is formed into pillars, and arches, and walls, with projections and turrets, all so uniquely put together, and yet so complicated, that a description is out of the question. Some of the party crawled through the openings in the sides of the wall, when it had cooled after an eruption. It throws an immense volume of water sixty feet in the air, and sometimes acts three or four times a day, though irregular in its eruptions. Two hundred yards from here, near the bank of Firehole River, is the Giant Geyser, which is the grandest and most gigantic fountain in the basin, and, as far as yet discovered, in the world. We had just left the Grotto, on our way to camp, and were resting in the cool shade of some intervening trees, not far away, when it began to give signs of an eruption, thus affording us a splendid opportunity to witness its movements.

This geyser is one of a group of three orifices or craters, all in a row and in close proximity, together with a small vent just off to one side, six inches in diameter, from which jets of steam are almost constantly emitted, much in the manner of the discharge of steam from the escape-pipe of a steam-engine, and with about the same regularity. They are all situated on a slight elevation about seventy-five or one hundred yards in diameter. The Giant is of course the principal one, and constitutes the centre of attraction. Its crater has been compared, in appearance, to the base of a broken horn, but for my life I could liken it to nothing that I had ever seen, save the stump of a hollow sycamore-tree of gigantic proportions, the top of which had been torn off in a storm. It rises ten or twelve feet above the platform, with a diameter of eight or ten feet at the top, with five feet cavity. One side is broken in—torn off, perhaps, by an unusually terrific eruption. It swells out irregularly at the base just like the roots of a huge tree; the grayish silica crust represents the bark of the sycamore, while the cavity is carved into numerous little grooves, and stained with various minerals, giving it a dark coating, reminding you of the decayed part of the inside of an old stump. But it changes its appearance as you approach, and look down into its depths. The angry gurgling of the water can be heard at all times many feet below, and occasionally the agitation is so great that it is thrown out over the top of the crater, together with volumes of rising steam.

All of the cavities are connected below and belong to the same system, thus giving the appearance of a wonderful engine, requiring almost a supernatural power to set it in motion. The machinery is rather complicated, and, after we hear the usual internal throbbings, as of Pluto's firemen dropping wood into a gigantic fiery furnace, it requires some little time to get things under headway. The first thing I observed when it gave signs of action was the cessation of the little steam-jet, when the geyser nearest it began to surge at a fearful rate, throwing a great volume of water to an altitude of twenty or thirty feet. It played but a moment, and the next one went through a similar operation, when, as if ashamed of their significant failures to rise in the world, or in honor of the grand chief of the realm who was about to appear, they all retired from the scene of action and became quiescent. Then, with a terrible rushing and rumbling below, with a powerful effort and fearful heavings that caused the very earth to groan, and seemed sufficient to tear the solid walls of the crater into a thousand atoms, the Giant came forth in the majesty of his mighty power. A volume of boiling water, the size of the nozzle of the crater, was projected to a great altitude, the action being repeated several times. Then for a moment all was quiet. Thinking it only a feint, we attempted to approach the orifice and make investigations, when we were met by an immense volume of steaming water, as if just from one of Hecate's caldrons, causing another disorderly retreat. It now commenced in earnest, and we surely witnessed one of the grandest displays of water-works ever beheld by mortal eyes. The fountains of the great deep seemed literally to have been broken up and turned loose again upon our sinful world. A steady column of water, graceful, majestic, and vertical, except as swayed by the passing breezes, was by rapid and successive impulses impelled upward above the steam until reaching the marvelous height of more than two hundred feet. At first it appeared to labor in raising the immense volume, which seemed loath to start on its heavenward tour, but now it was with perfect ease that the stupendous column was held to its place, the water breaking into jets and returning in glittering showers to the basin. The steam ascended in dense volumes for thousands of feet, when it was freighted upon the wings of the wind and borne away in clouds. The fearful rumble and confusion attending it were as the sound of distant artillery, the rushing of many horses to battle, or the roar of a fearful tornado. It commenced to act at 2 P.M., and continued for an hour and a half, the latter part of which it emitted little else but steam rushing upward from its chambers below, of which, if controlled, there is enough to run an engine of wonderful power. I advanced and stood near enough on the windward side to cast large masses of silica into the ascending volume, which were hurled with force many feet into the air. The waving to and fro of such a gigantic fountain when the column is at its highest—

"Tinseled o'er in robes of varying hues,"

and glistening in the bright sunlight which adorns it with the glowing colors of many a gorgeous rainbow—affords a spectacle so wonderful and grandly magnificent, so overwhelming to the mind, that the ablest attempt at description gives the reader who has never witnessed such a display but a feeble idea of its glory. Our entire party were perfectly wild with enthusiasm. We could not suppress emotion, but shouted and cheered till out of breath, and some fired revolvers and guns in the air, so great was the excitement in the presence of such a display. Every person in the basin—thirty-four in number—was soon on the ground, and lawyers, judges, professors, farmers, merchants, miners, and philosophers, were all alike filled with enthusiasm by the magnificent spectacle. A perfect river of water equal to the volume of the Firehole rushed down the slope; and in our excitement to get a view from every point of vision, we several times slightly tested its temperature by a misstep, landing us half-way to our boot-tops in the steaming flood. Every one thought the column two hundred and fifty feet high, though we had no means of measuring it. Its form is conical, much like the Faithful, and the action much the same, though that is not worthy of comparison in volume, length of time in action, and grandeur of appearance. It generally plays about once in twenty-four or twenty-nine hours, as nearly as yet ascertained. What an inconceivable power! what wonderful machinery to control it, in order to sustain such a river-volume at such an altitude, for even one hour! and then what a furnace and boiler, to generate steam to repeat it every twenty-four!

Having seen but half the geysers in action, and though desirous of staying a week among them, nevertheless I returned to camp, feeling amply compensated for all my trouble and travel, and ready to take my homeward march at any time, happy with the soul-enrapturing exhibitions which it had been my privilege to behold.

CHAPTER XIII.

Sunrise Eruptions.—Moonlight.—Firelight.—Sleeping among the Geysers.—A Californian.—The Name Geyser.—Geysers of Iceland.—Queries answered.—Breaking Through.—Theory of Geyser-Eruption.—In Camp.

THERE are hundreds of springs in the basin, all differing more or less in some particular. There are about twenty regularly acting, of which those mentioned in the last chapter are the principal ones. On a calm, clear morning, at or just before sunrise, when all the springs are sending up their columns of steam of every magnitude, and all boiling and fussing and splashing away, as if trying each to attract the greatest share of attention, and while one or two of the larger geysers are piercing the heavens with their stupendous columns, the basin presents a lively and interesting spectacle.

The eruptions as witnessed by moonlight are truly sublime, though deprived of much of their glory, as it is difficult to distinguish between water and steam. Some of the party built bonfires and watched the eruptions by firelight, which were very fine, giving the rising volumes the appearance of fiery liquid hurled forth from the crater of a volcano.

It is not the most quiet and agreeable place for sleeping. One is frequently disturbed during the night by the alarming detonations and subterranean thunder, making an almost constantly rumbling noise as of heavy machinery in motion, the come and go of ponderous freight-trains, the hiss and rush of escaping steam, and the loud plash of falling torrents, as the geysers, the ever-vigilant sentinels on the outposts of old Pluto's infernal regions, sound the alarm and spout forth in the darkness. This is more sensibly realized by sleeping on the ground, and, rest assured, the sensations are not always of the most desirable character.

It is conceded that the geysers of this region surpass anything of the kind in the known world—in number, in the volume of water discharged, in frequency and length of time in action, and the enormous height to which the up-rushing volumes are impelled by the internal forces at work.

While on a public conveyance recently, I met with a Californian. Though not a "Forty-niner," yet he exhibited the peculiarities often ascribed to the inhabitants of the "Golden State." The big trees and the wonderful cataracts were discussed, when he remarked, "We also have some remarkable curiosities in our State, called geysers."

"How high do your geysers spout their water?" I asked.

"About *four feet*," he replied, with great self-complacency, as though he thought that surpassed anything of the kind in the western hemisphere. He had never been to the National Park.

The term geyser (pronounced *ghi-ser*) is of Icelandic origin, signifying *rager* or *roarer*, and was applied to that wonderful group of spouting springs in Iceland, discovered in the fifteenth century, and until recently supposed to be the only springs of the kind in existence. I remember well how I was thrilled by reading an account of them by a traveler when I was a mere boy. There are but two of importance in the group. Their manner of action is much the same as that here described, but does not begin to compare with the wonderful exhibitions of the

Giant and Grand Geysers, sending their immense volumes hundreds of feet into the air.

Were I a scientist, I would speak at length of the causes at work producing these remarkable eruptions; though I am persuaded that a detail of all the wonderful phenomena of geyser. action, the various combination of gases generating heat and decomposing minerals, the mysterious processes of carrying them upward and working them into the inexplicably complicated geyser-tubes, requiring perhaps hundreds of years to perfect them, would take more space than the design of this work will permit. I refer the reader to the works of Tyndall, Bunsen, and other scientists, who have discussed these questions at length.

However, in order to satisfy, if possible, the minds of many querists who may never visit this region, I venture a few observations. I have been asked a hundred times, and by many who read my published account of a trip to the geysers, if the water thrown from the geysers is cold or *hot*. I answer most emphatically that it is as hot as it can be made.

Another asks, "Do they spout all the time?"

Of course not; for the eruptions are only caused by the discharge of steam confined in the vast heated chambers below, seeking an outlet through these valves, which discharge takes place periodically.

Another wants to know, "Were you not frightened at the underground thunderings, and afraid lest the earth should open at some place and let you drop into these boiling caldrons?"

I reply that, although a sensation of fear occasionally steals over me, yet, knowing the apparent solidity of the surface at most places, the great depth at which the reservoirs are located, and seeing so many pass safely over, such fears are soon dispelled. There are no signs of any recent explosions, or blow-ups, though now and then some adventurous fellow breaks through into the steaming mud or scalding water. One party of horsemen were fording the Firehole River, when the crust gave way under the horses' feet, and it seemed that the "bottom of the river" was indeed falling out. They escaped unhurt.

A Catholic priest was standing near a hot spring, when the crust gave way, and let him into the seething caldron. The accident would doubtless have proved fatal, but that a strong man who was at his side, and happened to be standing on solid ground, seized him by the collar and saved him from a horrible death. Though he escaped without any injury whatever, imagine his surprise at the appearance in an Eastern paper of a vivid account of his untimely death, together with an illustration showing a party of men dragging the lifeless body of a monk "all shaven and shorn," and attired in priestly robes, from one of the geysers! He still asserts that it is a mistake, notwithstanding the statements of the newspapers to the contrary.

Other inquisitive souls will still ask: "Is there any fire about there?" "What causes the heat?" "Are there evidences of volcanic action up there?" etc.

I saw no fire, only that which we ourselves kindled, and no marks of the action of real fire. There are convincing evidences that this whole region was once the scene of wonderful volcanic activities; and many think that the geysers only exhibit these activities in their last stages; that the heat is produced by these fires still burning far down in the bowels of the earth. My own opinion is, that far below the surface there are vast reservoirs or vacuums, the walls of which are heated by contact with the various minerals which abound in inexhaustible quantities, combining in every conceivable proportion, and thus creating numerous gases. The water, coming from the mountains and seeping through the earth, constantly flowing into these gigantic boilers, is quickly heated, rapidly generating steam, which soon acquires such force by confinement that it seeks an outlet. This can only be effected by the removal of the water intervening between it and the valve or aperture through which it must pass. As it expands, the vast body of water is gradually raised in the geyser-tube. As the volume is constantly increasing, and as it is raised higher, this makes the pressure greater on the steam, which now, acquiring almost irresistible force, breaks forth from its confinement, and in its upward rush carries with it the boiling volumes of water to a stupendous height, producing the geyser-eruption in all its matchless glory and splendor.

The water being removed, the steam escaping, quiet ensues, while preparations are made for another display. Thus the action is repeated from day to day, and from year to year, and even from century to century. The projectile force, the amount of water discharged, and the intervals between eruptions, depend largely upon the extent of the reservoirs, the quantity of water flowing in, the amount of heat, and the length of time required to "get up steam." The appearance and beauty of the fountain, of course, depend much upon the particular shape of the tube and of the orifice at the top.

Whenever railroads come within reach, or even passable wagon and stage roads are completed through the Park, this will become a favorite place of resort for people from every part of the world, though I prefer going in true pioneer style on horseback, with a pack-horse on which to carry provisions and baggage. A wagon-road is now completed from Virginia City up the Madison to the Lower Basin. But don't go until you can make the grand rounds, for the geysers, in all their glory, are only part of the wonders of the National Park.

While here we met with persons from various portions of

the Territory, among them a number of friends; and quite a sociable time we had the two evenings spent in the basin. After the sight-seeing of the day was over, we gathered around our brilliant camp-fire, and passed the time relating incidents and anecdotes of a pleasant character; while Miss Clark, a young lady from Chicago, with vocal gifts that all admired, charmed us with some excellent music, presenting quite a contrast as the charming melodies floated out upon the night-wind, and mingled with the hissing reports of a hundred noisy, spouting springs, the wild, weird appearance of everything adding greatly to the novelty of the surroundings.

From the geysers to the Yellowstone Lake there are two routes—one leading up the Firehole River, and crossing the divide, striking the lake-shore, fifteen or twenty miles from the outlet, which route, however, is heavily timbered most of the way, and quite difficult to travel, owing to the fallen timber lying across the trail. The other trail returns by the Lower Basin, thence across to Muddy Geyser, and up the west bank of Yellowstone River to the lake.

CHAPTER XIV.

Homeward bound.—Our Caravan.—Novel Way of Traveling.—Variety the Spice of Life.—Cayuses.—"Bucking" Propensities.—Noble Animals.—Camp-Life: its Pleasures.—A Pleasant Party.—Dream fulfilled.—Narrow Escape of "the Judge."

On the morning of September 1st the animals were driven in, saddled, and camp-equipage stowed away carefully on the pack-horses; and just as Old Faithful, a geyser so much admired by all, and the first to welcome us to the basin by a display of her powers, was now honoring us with a farewell exhibition, we mounted and commenced our homeward march, nearly thirty persons, all on horseback, with about twenty pack-animals— quite a caravan, and rather a novel scene, too, to one not accustomed to mountain-life, and a stranger to this mode of traveling. It is rather amusing to see the little ponies (commonly known in the mountains as *cayuses*) trudging along with the great, bulky loads on their backs, now wading through almost fathomless swamps, winding their way among the densely-crowded pines, or ingeniously working a passage amid a network of fallen timber so complicated as often to present difficulties almost insurmountable. It is wonderful to see the caution they will use in choosing the trail and avoiding contact with the trees, as though they felt themselves responsible for the safe delivery at night of the charge commmitted to them. Sometimes, however, patience gives way under the pressure, the virtue of forbearance is forgotten, and novelty and humor are lost in vexation, as you are called to urge your way through such a trackless wilderness; though now and then an amusing incident occurs, as a man gets caught in a net of fallen trunk or overhanging boughs, loses his hat or part of his clothing, or perhaps is brought by awkwardness or the sudden gyrations of his cayuse to his all-fours, face-foremost in the mud, which, though far from being laughable to him, furnishes amusement to those more fortunate, reviving the spirits of all, and verifying the truth of the old adage that "variety is the spice of life."

Useful animals these little cayuses are, and perfectly harmless when brought fully under the "influences of civilization;" but woe to him who becomes the owner, and thus the *victim*, of one not properly domesticated! Sometimes when things go wrong, or their cayuse nature is revived by a day's rest or a good mess of bunch-grass, they commence a performance usually known out West as "bucking"—placing the head between the forelegs and rearing and plunging, going up before, then behind, throwing their pedal extremities in every way but in their natural position, or jumping high in the air, having the happy faculty of bringing all their feet stoutly to the earth at the same instant. Then they take them up as soon, and whirl round and round until they are relieved of their burden, or completely exhausted in the attempt. They are expert at the business, which, by-the-way, is a natural propensity of theirs. The new-comer has never gone the round of misfortunes that mortals are heir to, nor become fully initiated into the experience of a mountaineer's life, until he has been tumbled promiscuously a few times from the "hurricane-deck of a bucking cayuse."

But these small horses are the main dependence of the frontier. They are stout, tough, and ambitious—will endure any amount of hardship, and subsist upon bunch-grass alone. If a stampede is on hand, a long ride or drive to make, a load to draw, Indians to chase, a prospecting expedition or a trip to Wonderland before you, cayuses are brought into immediate demand. There is no animal that does more service or endures more hardship than he, yet none more severely used. He will frequently carry a man a hundred miles in a day; and yet, after the journey, which an American horse perhaps would not make, is ended, he is turned upon the range to "rustle" for his food, with the remark that "he is *only a cayuse*, anyhow!" And, considering the way he is broken to the saddle or harness, who would expect him not to "buck?" Let run at will upon the prairies until of mature age, having never seen a halter, perhaps, he is driven into the *corral*, lassoed round the neck, "snubbed" up to a post, choked down and blindfolded; a great heavy saddle is "sinched" upon him so tightly that he can hardly breathe; a Spanish bridle with heavy bit is put on him; then, just as he rises to his feet, a man springs into the saddle, the blindfold is withdrawn, the gate thrown open, and with a pair of great, jingling, jagged spurs digging him in the sides, frightened out of his senses and suffering with pain, he goes forth at full speed and comes back "broke"—*for the time.* No wonder he "bucks." He wouldn't be worth a cent if he did not.

But I will not apologize too much, for more than once have I been the unfortunate and unhappy victim of these creatures while exhibiting their striking propensities in a very forcible manner, and just when I was not expecting it, when thinking there was no earthly cause for such conduct. They are not at all careful where or how they leave you, and you generally come down in the most unfavorable position conceivable—on your head or the flat of your back, and maybe right in a bed of prickly pears. Pray to be delivered from such misfortunes when you come West!

Captain W. W. Delacy, in his account of a prospecting tour up the Snake River in 1863, published in "Contributions to the Historical Society of Montana," vol. i., in which tour, by-the-way, he claims to have passed through the Lower Geyser Basin, refers humorously to an adventure with a cayuse. It is characteristic, and quite amusing. He says: "I had a white, bob-tailed cayuse (usually called Muggins), who had the peculiarity of having one eye black and the other of a very light blue. When you looked at him on one side, he had a very obstinate and devilish look, as if he was up to any mischief (and so he was). Looking at him on the other, he seemed a very good natured, steady old horse, with a tendency toward religion. He had other peculiarities besides these, among which was, that when you tried to lead him, he wouldn't go anywhere, if he could help it, and, if you let him go loose, you could not catch him under an hour.

"This evening, as the wind was cold, and he had been good for a long time, he concluded that the time had come to distinguish himself. He was just before me, and, looking around, he cocked his black eye at me, as much as to say, 'Look out for squalls!' and gave two or three preliminary kicks, which threw off the pack, which he met with his heels, and sent the coffee-pot, frying-pan, a piece of elk, a chunk of bread, and other miscellaneous articles, into the air. He then galloped around, scattering the rest of the kit over the prairie, and, when he ascertained that there was no more mischief to be done, he let himself be caught, and, when I came up, he turned his blue eye on me with such an expression of contrite humility and self-reproach, that I had not the heart to give him the thrashing he richly deserved, and repacked him in silence and went on my way."

At another place in his journal he says: "As my pack-horse, who was an independent animal, and had notions of his own, declined being driven, I was compelled to drag him, and, for that purpose, had taken a hitch with the lariat around the horn of the saddle. The pack becoming disarranged, I dismounted to fix it, and, while doing this, my riding-horse commenced capering around, and in some way got the rope across the lock of the gun, and caused it to go off directly toward me, the ball passing just over my head. There is always some consolation in the worst misfortunes, however, and, when I got over my scare, I felt very thankful that he had not fired the other barrel at me, which was loaded with buck-shot."

However, our road is not all so rough, nor misfortunes so numerous, after all. Much of the way is through an open country, with delightful landscape-views before the eye, yet abounding with picturesque beauties, making the trip altogether quite pleasant when the weather is mild. The day is usually spent in observing the curiosities along the route. Toward evening, as the sun is approaching the towering summits of the western mountains, the expedition halts, usually in some lovely park by the side of a sparkling mountain-stream, when the horses, relieved of their burdens, are lariated, hoppled, or turned loose upon the grass. A cheerful fire, made of dry pine, is soon blazing, and, while some are shooting grouse or ducks, or looking out for elk or deer, and others fishing for trout, the evening repast is prepared, for which you are sure to have a relish. Supper over, the tents are stretched, and beds, robes, mattresses, or blankets, as the case may be, are spread upon the ground or on pine-boughs or bunch-grass, and made ready for the night. The party then usually gather in a group around the fire, and discuss the curiosities observed during the day, or all listen attentively to anecdotes or some thrilling narration of Western adventure, when all lay them down, and sweetly sleep till morning.

It is amazing to see the economy practised by the mountaineer in the make-up of the culinary department. With a frying-pan, camp-kettle, and a coffee-pot, his supply of cooking utensils is complete, and, with a few staple articles in the way of groceries, he will fare sumptuously every day. You would be surprised at the variety of *dishes* that he will serve up even from a limited larder.

Our cook was proud of his expertness in the culinary art, and one morning concluded to have cakes—commonly known among the mountaineers as "slapjacks"—for breakfast. When browned on one side, with a quick, artistic movement he would flip them up in the frying-pan, and turn them with all ease, and with no little satisfaction to himself. He called upon the ladies and the entire party who sat by the fire to witness an exhibition of his skill. "Just see how I can flip 'em over!" he said. All eyes being turned, he gave his arm a twitch—up went the cakes, whirling over and over. But, alas for John's pride! his nerves were too highly strung; he overdid himself, and spoiled it all. Down came the cakes, missing the frying-pan and falling into the fire, to the infinite amusement of all present, except the mortified cook, whose countenance was soon below zero. He repeated the operation afterward with better success; but never desired spectators, nor permitted criticism.

On the return-trip my good-natured traveling-companion and myself would usually construct a *wickiup* of pine-boughs, which was almost as comfortable as a house. However, one stormy night, when we most needed a covering, we were compelled to seek shelter under a single blanket, stretched across a pole over our bed, and, strange as it appears, we slept soundly till morning. There is nothing like "getting used to things."

In our party, on the return-trip, were W. H. Todd, of Helena; Hon. Hiram Knowles, one of the Associate Judges of Montana; and a young man by the name of Robbins, from New York. These gentlemen were congenial traveling-companions, and added greatly to the pleasure of the journey. Traveling in company with us was also a party of very pleasant gentlemen from Deer-Lodge City, among whom were Hon. Granville Stewart, one of the old pioneers, and now an honored citizen of Montana; Prof. Egbert Smith, and others, who are remembered with pleasure. We generally camped in close proximity, and passed the evening hours around one camp-fire.

While in the Park we also on several occasions were thrown in company with Colonel W. F. Sanders, who, with his wit and constant flow of good-nature, contributed much to the life and merriment of the entire party.

There is no mode of life better calculated to develop every trait of human character than camp-life. Every virtue will be surely and severely tested, and every vice is certain to show itself. Wit, wisdom, humor, cheerfulness, patience, and industry, are in demand, and their opposites at a discount. If a man is lazy, fretful, or disagreeable, it soon shows itself around the camp-fire. And what can be more disagreeable than the strifes and bickerings of fellow-travelers, who hitherto were on the most intimate terms? But they are of frequent occurrence. Persons who have been warm friends for years will often fall out and become bitter enemies the first week in camp. Nothing, however, is more pleasurable than traveling in such a country as this, with a genial party like ours, where each is concerned for the pleasure of the others. Long will we remember the many happy hours spent around the camp-fire with our traveling-companions, and more than once will we meet and recount the incidents of this eventful tour.

We camped at night near the source of a small stream, the waters of which find their way into the Madison. The latter stream is one of the largest of the three rivers that unite near Gallatin City to form the Missouri. We were, therefore, on the head-waters of the " Big Muddy " itself. I remember, when but a small boy, and living on the bank of the Missouri, which at that place is a mighty river, of a dream in which I was wafted on fairy wings away to the source of that wonderful stream, where, with one or two boyish companions, I was leaping across the miniature water-course—there only a brook—with great delight.

Afterward, as I traced on the big map that hung on the wall the meanderings of the grand old river to where it appeared to lose itself among its wild environs, I thought how strange and foolish the dream, and how absurd the ideas that it awakened in my youthful mind! I could but think of it all, as I stepped across the little rivulet that rippled along in its course so near our camp; and more than once I have stood upon some high mountain overlooking the thousands of tributaries that help to swell the volume of one of the grandest rivers of the world, or in my journey dismounted and leaped across some little brooklet not far from the summit of the Rocky Mountains, with a strange sense of boyish dreams fulfilled, and long-cherished ambition gratified.

Ascending and descending the rugged steep along the trail are often quite laborious, and it is frequently found advisable to dismount and walk over the worst places. But our jolly friend Judge G——, who rode a hired horse, and being quite corpulent, too, persisted in riding every step of the way, up hill and down. While going up a very steep mountain the saddle slipped back to a place not the most agreeable to the sensitive cayuse that he was riding. The animal began to make forcible efforts to "raise" the judge, which, if successful, would have been followed by rather a sudden "letting down." He called lustily for help, which a moment later would have been unavailing. But he was rescued from the threatened and much-dreaded calamity, and the cavalcade moved forward.

Among those persons whom we met on the way to and through the Park—who are remembered with pleasure—are Col. Deimling, Pat Largey, D. P. Newcomer, Charley Aspling, Mr. Frazier, Mrs. George McFaddin, Miss Lena McFaddin, John Hildebrand, Judge Symmes, Bart Henderson, Mr. Daly and family, Mr. Fitzgerald and family, C. J. Baronette, Fred Bottler, of Yellowstone Valley, and E. H. Chrisman, photographer.

YELLOWSTONE LAKE.

CHAPTER XV.

Trip to the Yellowstone Lake.—Description of the Lake.—Dimensions.—Depth.—Huge Bear-Tracks.—A Cold Bath.—Swans and other Water-fowls.—Swarms of Trout.—Intestinal Affection.—Not hungry for Fish.—Numerous Islands.—Mr. Stevenson's Visit.—Wild Beasts.—Once trod by the Red-Man.—Tradition.—Hot Spring in the Lake.—Cooking Fish.—Mountaineer's Idea of the Lake.—Conjecture.—Mr. Everts's Adventure.—Is lost, and wanders for Thirty-seven Days.—Lives on Thistle-Roots.—Attacked by a Mountain-Lion.—Thrilling Account.—Miraculous Deliverance.—Splendid Place in which to spend the Summer.—Mountains.—Inspiring Scenes.

ON our return, we traveled part of the way on the trail made going over, encamping in a clump of pines near Muddy Geyser, on the banks of the Yellowstone. The following morning, the 3d of September, after a long search for our animals, which had again played truant, and were not brought in till noon, I mounted my horse, and, after a delightful ride of six miles southward along the densely-wooded banks of the placid river, fed by a thousand silvery streamlets that trickle down from the mountains, and observing now and then a flock of graceful swans playing upon the emerald-tinted surface of the Yellowstone, we were suddenly ushered from the dense forest, shaded by overhanging mountains, into a delightful, grassy park, where, before our astonished and wondering eyes, spread out, in all its native beauty and loveliness, the famed Yellowstone Lake, which is far from being the least of the attractions found on our "rambles in Wonderland." It is a wonderful sheet of water, fifteen miles in width, and estimated to be twenty or twenty-five in length. Its shores are indented with bays and inlets which are fringed with pine-forests, with now and then a meadow-like opening, to add to the variety and give greater beauty to the scene.

The enthusiastic Langford, the superintendent of the park, pays the following handsome tribute to this inland sea:

"Secluded amid the loftiest peaks of the Rocky Mountains, possessing strange peculiarities of form and beauty, this watery solitude is one of the most attractive objects in the world. Its southern shore, indented with long, narrow inlets, not unlike the frequent fiords of Iceland, bears testimony to the awful upheaval and tremendous force of the elements which resulted in its erection. The long pine-crowned promontories, stretching into it from the base of the hills, lend new and charming features to an aquatic scene full of novelty and splendor. Islands of emerald hue dot its surface, and a margin of sparkling sand forms its setting. The winds, compressed in their passage through the mountain-gorges, lash it into a sea as terrible as the fretted ocean, covering it with foam. But now it lay before us calm and unruffled, save as the gentle wavelets broke in murmurs along the shore. Water, one of the grandest elements of scenery, never seemed so beautiful before."

This picture may appear overdrawn, yet it is in harmony with our own emotions when we first stood on the shore, and must agree, in part, with the sentiments awakened in every Nature-admiring beholder. I was most agreeably disappointed in the beauty of the scene, and, though lingering for hours, feasting my eyes upon the enchanting beauties made strange and novel by the wild, weird appearance of the surroundings, at last turned my steps homeward with regrets that I could not stay longer.

This islet of water reposes upon the crown of our North American Continent, near the source of the three great rivers of the United States, at an altitude of nearly seven thousand five hundred feet, far above the loftiest clouds that cast their shadows over New England homes, or float in the azure sky of the sunny South. Its superficial area is three hundred square miles, and its greatest soundings are about three hundred feet. It has no inlets of note, save the Yellowstone, which runs through, and is its only outlet. This stream and a few small torrents that rush down from the mountains are its only feeders, it being principally supplied by the "eternal snows" from the lofty ranges environing it. At morning and evening, when the atmosphere is calm, and the bright sunlight falls upon the placid surface of emerald hue, in which is reflected the overarching canopy, the beholder is filled with admiring wonder, and in the midst of such awe-inspiring influences is tempted to bow the knee and worship at Nature's shrine. In the middle of the day, when the mountain-winds come down from their fastnesses, it assumes an appearance more in accordance with its wild surroundings. Its shape somewhat resembles that of an open hand, the long, narrow bays stretching out to the southward reminding you of the fingers. The shores sparkle with volcanic pebbles, carnelians, petrifactions, and numerous specimens, some of which are of great beauty.

But the first thing I noticed when I stepped upon the beach was the track of a huge bear, quite in accordance, thought I, with the surroundings, which for a while disturbed sentimental reflections, and, being alone, naturally enough caused me to adjust my fire-arms, so as to be ready, on short notice, for a reception by Bruin, upon whose dominions I was intruding. The water was so clear that, deceived in its temperature by that of the atmosphere, which was rather cool, I was tempted to go bathing, and swam out into the crystal depths fifty or sixty yards, and came back fully satisfied with one such adventure.

Numerous flocks of fowls of almost every species throng the shore and dot the surface; and I could but think what a quiet, safe retreat it is for them, where they can rear their young; but now their resort has been discovered, and already they begin to fall before the sharp crack of the hunter's rifle and the shrill report of the sportsman's fowling-piece. Beautiful swans, with snowy plumage and graceful form, may be seen here and there, while pelicans, gulls, geese, brants, and many kinds of ducks, abound.

The lake, as well as the river, literally swarms with speckled trout of great beauty, and some of excellent flavor, which are easily taken with hook and line. But most of them have some kind of an affection which destroys the satisfaction one would otherwise enjoy in eating them. The intestines are often covered with small worms, which are frequently found in the flesh, softening it, and giving the fish a sickly look. Some of our party, who were out of meat, insisted that they were "just as good as any fish," though, as I could not shut my eyes while eating, I happened not to be hungry for trout. This affection seems to characterize those only in the lake and above the Great Falls, and their existence constitutes a problem that the ichthyologist has not yet solved.

The surface of the lake is broken by the uprising of several small islands. The first explorers constructed a rude craft, in which they sailed over the lake and visited one or two of the principal islands. Mr. Stevenson found them covered with large pine-timber, abounding in dense jungles, the safe retreat of bears, mountain-lions, deer, and other game, the signs of which were but too evident. He found an arrow-head, which is good evidence that the island had been trodden by human beings, if never before by the white man. Doubtless "the noble red-man" roamed these forests in search of game, and paddled his canoe from island to island in gleeful sport, hundreds of years ago. The curiously-formed stones along the pebbly strand, in the old trapper's fancy, were the war-clubs, arrow-heads, and other utensils, of a strange class of beings, and doubtless originated the traditions afloat concerning a race of people who once inhabited this region, but are now extinct.

The explorers also made the complete circuit of this vast sheet of water, penetrating the trackless woods and fearful swamps, and encountering almost insuperable difficulties. The timber is so dense that every few years it is burned out, leaving the trunks standing until sufficiently dead, when they are swept by a violent wind, and piled up in every conceivable manner, presenting an obstruction that is quite trying to the patient, adventurous equestrian. They are called "fire-slashes."

In the basin around the lakes are numerous hot-spring deposits, and some of the springs are yet in action. At one place there is a white cone, almost surrounded by the water of the lake, projecting several feet above the surface, on the apex of which is a funnel-shaped crater, full of boiling water. You can stand on the formation and catch trout, and, without moving from your tracks, if cruel enough, can cook them without their removal from the line.

I remember hearing an old mountaineer tell of a lake, on the very summit of the Rocky Mountains, from which the water flowed into both oceans. I think he got it from Bridger, who used to talk of a "Two-World Lake." He thought it was the Yellowstone Lake, and accounted for the existence of salmon-trout in the Yellowstone River—the only place where this species abounds on the east of the mountains, though quite abundant in the waters of the Pacific slope—by their having ascended the streams on the other side to the lake, and then descended into this river. But, like many other conjectures, it has proved to be without foundation.

It was while exploring the shores of this lake that Mr. Everts was lost from his party, and soon became confused and strangely bewildered, losing his horse, which he said broke away from him, carrying with it his fire-arms and all his personal effects. His party searched diligently, but in vain. They also *cached* supplies, but he never found them. They were compelled to leave, as provisions were short, and thinking, too, that he had started homeward, and that they would overtake him; and he wandered about in this wilderness for *thirty-seven days*, without shelter and without food, save a few fish caught with a pin and the roots that he gathered in his wanderings, which were cooked in a hot spring. He saw game in abundance, but had not a weapon with him to take it, and narrowly escaped being torn to pieces by a mountain-lion, which made the forest echo with its hideous screams while it walked around the tree that he had ascended, lashing the ground with its tail. During a severe snow-storm his only couch was the warm crust near a hot spring, and a few pine-branches his only covering, his blankets having been left on the horse. In his reduced state he said that the members of his body seemed to be transformed into traveling-companions, which tantalized him with their hideous appearance and the demands they made upon him in his imaginary conversations with them. The stomach complained constantly of his diet—thistle-roots—and demanded better food; the legs complained of want of rest, and the arms of being overtaxed, while he was doing all he could for them; and they seemed absolutely to refuse to do anything toward helping themselves. He would strive to quiet them by promises of better times when they were at home. Fortunately, he had a field-glass, with which he obtained fire when the sun shone. Several times he was ready to give up in despair, when thoughts of the loved ones at home, and of how sad they would be, inspired him to continued efforts, nerving him with almost supernatural strength, thus enabling him to survive till his rescuers found him on a mountain near the Mammoth Springs. They had been sent out by his friends. He was found in a famished condition—a mere skeleton—but, with kind treatment, he recovered; and while we were on our trip we met him returning from a second tour to Wonderland, which doubtless was much more satisfactory. The story of his marvelous adventure and miraculous escape has been published, and is a most thrilling narrative.

Along the shores of this inland sea would be a delightful place to spend a summer, and I longed for a week's time to occupy myself in exploring its mysteries and enjoying its attractions, which are many.

The views from the tops of those snowy mountains over there to the southward must be overwhelmingly grand—standing almost on the crest of the world, up among the clouds, looking down upon the pinnacling summits of thousands of glistening "snowy minarets," vying in beauty and rivaling each the other for preëminence. Then, between, are the craggy, shelving sides, immense gorges, rounded knolls, and lonely defiles, with clusters of lesser buttes crowned with numerous, rusty-looking, breccia-like spiral summits, reminding one of the ruins of some ancient city with domes and castles, the remnants of departed glory and prosperity. There are a hundred lovely lakelets hid away in the dreary solitude. The steam curling up over the pines from innumerable vents gives the appearance of civilization; while far, far away to the east, west, north, and south, as far as the range of vision can be extended, are outlines of landscapes, and mountains melting away in the clouds as if uniting terrestrial with celestial glory, clothing things earthly with the tapestry of the heavenly world. Who is not inspired when amid the mountains?

I was once permitted in a mountain-scene to behold as perfect a picture of the journey of life and the outlines of the Celestial City as can ever be witnessed this side the New Jerusalem itself. The sky above me was almost obscured with intervening clouds, while down the river, at the lower end of the Gallatin Valley, was a dark, threatening cloud, extending across the valley and enshrouding the mountains on either side. It hung right over the Missouri River; was very low, and exceedingly threatening in its appearance. I had been thinking that day of the journey of the Israelites through the wilderness, and of how beautifully it illustrated the journey of life—

". . . . through the vale and the shadow,
Through sorrow, temptation, and care."

The picture before me was complete. The clouds often appear darker as we approach the river. But just then my eye passed between the descending showers of snow, which reminded me of the folds of a vast curtain closing for a moment and then opening again—and such a view! I never can forget it. Beyond the threatening cloud, and beyond the river, the sky was clear, and never before had it appeared so blue. The mountain, mantled with snow and dotted with pine-groves, ascended from the river in terraces, gradually receding, yet towering to a great height. The sun covered all with a flood of glory. The terraces, slopes, and shadows, resembled the walls, arches, and domes, of a beautiful city, with streets, mansions, and temples, burnished with gold, and skirted with fields and lovely landscapes. Bathed in the bright sunlight, it reminded me of the Celestial City itself. The effect was inspiring. I was overcome with emotion, and felt that "but thinly the vale intervened between the fair city and me." I was for the moment carried away, in spirit, from earth, and imagined myself on the "glittering strand," passing through the shining portals and up the "golden streets," meeting in my way the glorious inhabitants of the celestial region. It was a picture that will never fade from memory. And often while viewing a gorgeous sunset in the mountains, or feasting the eye upon a lovely landscape, the outlines—the "golden portals"—of the home of the soul, over there in the sweet by-and-by beyond the clouds and beyond the tomb, where the sun never sets and the clouds disappear forever, seem to appear in the distance.

No wonder the superstitious Blackfoot imagines that, from a place where such beauty and glory meet the enraptured vision, he can look over into the happy hunting-grounds.

It was one of the peaks of the Wind River range, away to the south of Yellowstone Lake, that Captain Bonneville ascended in his endeavor to cross that range, and of which he gives such a glowing description.

CHAPTER XVI.

Lake-Shore.—Hunting.—The Bear.—The Moose.—Mountain-Grouse.—"Fool-Hens."
—Sage-Chickens.—Panther or Mountain-Lion.—Lassoing a Bear.—Beaver.—
Their Homes.—Industry.—Desolation.—Charming Solitude.—Homeward
bound.—Camping in the Rain.—Return to Mammoth Springs.—The Parting.—
On to Bottler's Ranch.—Preaching on Sunday.—A Refreshing Time.—Indian
"Scare."—A Stampede.—Running for Life.—Arrival at Bozeman.—Cordial
Reunions.—Ample Compensation.

THE lake-shore and surrounding woodlands afford excellent opportunities for the sportsman to indulge his ruling propensity. Besides the myriads of water-fowl, abundance of wild game, such as deer, elk, moose, bear, mountain-lions, etc., is found in woodland, jungle, and park. The game is usually driven from the trail to more secluded regions, and cannot be found without hunting. You can have your choice, from the mountain-grouse that inhabit the fir-trees, to the panthers or bears that skulk in the jungle. The sensible mountaineer, however, will persist, when you talk of hunting, that he "hasn't lost any bar." These animals are quite plentiful in Montana and in the Park, and are often quite ferocious. Lewis and Clarke had many encounters with them, and record hair-breadth escapes from them. They seldom attack a man, however, except when they have young, or are wounded and pressed by their pursuers. But it is well at such times to "make yourself scarce." Many a poor man has *been* hunted, and compelled to seek refuge among the branches of a friendly tree, where he would often hang in suspense until relieved by his companions, or until his belligerent enemy would become disgusted with "such little business," and depart. Sometimes they will congregate in numbers and watch their frightened foe, who, in his rapid flight, has left his weapons on the field of battle, until the break of day. I have never seen any here save the grizzly, which are the most ferocious, a few of which I have met in my travels in the mountains. I usually offer them the road. Cinnamon and black bears also abound; but all of them are quick-scented and shy, and you scarcely ever meet with them in your rambles.

The most remarkable animal of these regions is the moose, and the most unearthly, hideous-looking monster that roams the mountains on four legs. He belongs to the elk family, though he is much larger; is covered with long, coarse, shaggy-looking hair, which in spring-time is nearly black; has a short thick neck, ugly head, much like that of a mule, small eye, ears like small saddle-skirts, which hang in a slouchy manner, with the most monstrous nose and upper lip, that hangs like a flap over the mouth, and dangles about quite amusingly when he is in motion. The male has large, ugly, palmated or web-like horns, which with his prodigious nose and lip complete the catalogue of astonishing proportions, constituting him the most uncomely animal of the West. His haunt is in the quiet, brushy, marshy glens of the mountains. He is easily approached and taken, if you have the "wind," and can see him before he starts. But, when once on the run, he is hard to capture, being on the alert for many hours after. The moose feeds upon willows, "larb," and various other shrubs and branches of trees. His usual gait is a trot, which will often surpass the speed of a fleet horse. When excited, the animal changes his gait to a most awkward lope, throwing his long legs promiscuously about, which greatly lessens its speed. The flesh is not sought after, save the nose, which constitutes quite a dish with the old mountaineer. "No accounting for tastes, you know."

Numerous flocks of mountain-sheep roam the "rugged steeps" and clamber among the rocks. They have heads and horns something like the sheep, though they are formed like the deer, being about the same size. The males have enormous horns. The flesh is delicious. They live among the rocks, and scamper over the cliffs, leaping from crag to crag with great alacrity. This is their haunt; and, when pursued, they at once flee to the rocks, where they find quite a safe retreat.

The mountains are full of grouse. They live among the fir-trees, and are easily captured. They generally sit until you are right upon them, when they start simultaneously with a fluttering, flapping sound, often annoying, if you are in search of larger game, as this is a note of alarm to the elk or watchful deer. But they often perch upon the dead timber, where they remain until you can shoot the entire flock. Splendid game they are for the inexperienced gunner; for, if you miss the first time, they kindly sit still and give you another shot. They will often sit or run by the road-side, and the driver slays them with his whip, or knocks them over with a club. For this remarkable trait they are frequently known as "fool-hens"—a suggestive title. The flesh is white and delicious. The sage-hen is much larger—nearly as large as the domestic turkey. It is found among the sage-bushes, the leaves of which constitute much of its food, giving the meat a dark color and a sagy taste, especially in the fall of the year.

I mention the mountain-lions, whose lairs are found in the jungles and caves of these mountains. They are a species of panther, and many think them to be the same as the panthers of the States. They are not numerous, and live mostly in the "secret corners of the earth." They are seldom seen, and are not considered ferocious, except when followed to their haunts, though Mr. Everts says he was pursued by one of them. They are occasionally captured by the expert hunter. A friend of mine says he caught one far away from the timber—upon a journey, I suppose—attacked it, when it showed a cowardly spirit, refused to fight, and became an easy prey. This was equal to the feat, accomplished in Madison Valley, of *lassoing a bear and killing him with stones*. The day being warm and pleasant, Bruin had sauntered forth on a visit or journey to another range. When far out upon the prairie, he was espied by a denizen of the valley, who gave the alarm and gathered a *posse*; and, the day being exceedingly hot, Mr. Bruin soon succumbed to his captors, who in their great haste, strange to say, had forgotten their guns, and literally, so it is said, stoned him to death—partly in revenge for his cruelty in chasing their friends when out hunting, and partly for the nightly visits he had made to their pig-sties and calf-pens, though mostly, I suppose, out of sheer prejudice against the Bruin family.

But we cannot leave this place before speaking of another very notable little animal of a species so numerous along the rivers, swamps, and lakes, of the mountains—the beaver. The proofs of the industry and untiring energy of these little creatures are found everywhere along the streams in the number of fallen trees, and the thousands of ingeniously-constructed dams spanning the smaller water-courses. Their long, sharp teeth enable them to fell good-sized trees, the limbs of which are carried and placed in position, when they are plastered with mud, the industrious little workers using their broad, flat tails for the double purpose of "hod" and "trowel." They are most ingenious mechanics and untiring in their labors. If their work is destroyed, they go at once to the task of rebuilding. They are very shy, for you seldom get sight of them while at work, and very difficult to entrap by one not thoroughly acquainted with their habits. But the thousands of broken and unrepaired dams, ruins of vacant homes, the half-notched trees, where no one was left to finish the work, tell the sad havoc that has been made among these noble and valuable little animals by the ingenious trapper, and only repeat the story of the desolation that will in a few years pervade the now densely-inhabited "beaver-towns" amid these remote mountains and valleys. They are very numerous on many of the tributaries putting into the Yellowstone Lake.

But, to return to the lake-shore, from which I have wandered so far. I strolled along the pebbly strand for hours, gathering specimens, meditating upon the wonders and beauties of the place, and watching and listening to the requiem of the wavelets as they broke in murmurs along the shore, until reminded by the lengthening shadows that night would soon find me alone in this desert wilderness, as all my companions had gone. Taking leave of this charming solitude, which is to-day associated in my mind with some of the delightful memories of the past, thinking of the busied multitudes of pleasure-seekers that will, in a few years, throng these shores, and almost hearing the plash of oars, mingled with the voices of merry tourists, that will ring out upon the atmosphere, as beautiful yachts and fleet sail-boats, filled with gleeful parties of delighted people, will be seen playing upon the smooth surface, I rode back to camp, when, after our evening repast, followed by the usual chat, and a salute from the noisy, splashing, turbulent Muddy Geyser, I retired to rest in the rude bower of pine-branches to dream of the pleasures and comforts of home. Next day we continued our journey homeward. We spent the Sabbath at Mammoth Springs, having been out from this place just thirteen days. Here, with regret, I parted from my excellent traveling-companions, my associations with whom will always be remembered only with feelings of pleasure.

On Monday I returned to Bottler's ranch on the Yellowstone, where, as the Indians were reported troublesome between there and Bozeman, I remained a week with kind friends, spending the time most delightfully in visiting during the week, and preaching on Sunday to a respectable audience in Mr. Bottler's new residence. I took the names of five persons for membership in the church, which number would be greatly increased if they could only have a regular pastor. It was a refreshing time, as minister and people for the first time, away here in this apparent wilderness on the banks of the Yellowstone, in plain view of scores of Indian lodges, met to worship God together. We felt that the Lord of hosts was with us, and that our hearts were refreshed with the baptism of the Holy Spirit. Long will I remember that occasion and those dear friends.

I found the inhabitants of the valley greatly excited about the Indians just at this time. A party of Sioux had made a dash on the Crow Agency after my visit there, killing two men, and had been seen skulking in the mountains toward Bozeman. A raid was expected nightly, and all was confusion. An old gentleman and his wife, living alone in a cabin, hearing repeated reports of a gun on the mountain one day, fled for dear life, with surprising speed, for persons of their age, to the next house, shouting, "Indians! Indians!" as they went, thinking the red-skins were right on them, and that the next moment they would be scalped. Of course the neighbors were alarmed, and stood at their doors with loaded guns. They were somewhat relieved, however, when they saw a man coming down the road with a half-dozen grouse, which he had been shooting with his revolver, and which had caused the alarm.

As the majority of the Crow warriors had gone on their buffalo-hunt, and the Sioux were known to be in this region, it was policy to be well prepared, and I confess to a little "scare" myself as I returned to Bozeman on Monday. Just at the place where the Indians were supposed to be, I saw a party of horsemen, with some loose animals, approaching, and, being but two of us together, though well armed, for a few moments we were kept in anxious suspense. We were greatly relieved when the horsemen were found to be friendly—whites.

One of the most thrilling incidents related in the history of Western adventure, showing the true character of the Crow Indians, and displaying the daring and true bravery of Montana's early pioneers, occurred some distance below the Bozeman Crossing, on this valley, early in the spring of 1863. A party of fifteen men, under Captain James Stuart, were on their way from Bannock City, to explore the Lower Yellowstone and Big-Horn Valleys, and to prospect the adjacent mountains for gold. One evening, when in camp on the north bank of the Yellowstone, a large party of Crow Indians made their appearance and came into camp. They soon became insolent, and would steal every thing they could lay their hands upon. Early next morning the men, fearing trouble, began to saddle their horses and make arrangements for any emergency that might arise. But the Indians would not let them bridle a horse, and began to take possession themselves, even quarreling among themselves as to who should have the best horses.

Presently the brave captain of the little band, catching the head chief of the Crows off his guard and away from his men, leveled his unerring rifle at the chief's heart, fiercely reproached him for his bad faith to the whites, and told him to " signal his warriors off, or he would send him to his last hunting-ground." Every man at the same instant covered a savage with his gun or revolver, while their robes fell from their shoulders, and their guns were leveled in the faces of the whites in return. The crisis had come, and the suspense must have been awful, as that little band of prospectors, hundreds of miles from reënforcements or relief, stood surrounded by twice their number of savages, whose snake-like, fiendish eyes were turned upon them, and their guns cocked and just waiting for the order to fire. But the old chief saw that he was gone if a hand moved, and he weakened, signaling his warriors away. So great was the relief from the fearful suspense of a moment before, that one of the men threw up his hat and shouted with laughter. This so aroused a young chief, a "tall, fine-looking young warrior, and as brave as Julius Cæsar," who was pale with rage, because the old chief had not signaled the fight, that he came up and put his finger on his white brother's nose, then on his own, and then on both their guns, and pointed to one side. It was a plain challenge for a duel. For a moment the party forgot their danger, laughed heartily, and urged their comrade to "go in," saying that he could "get away with him," but he could not see the point, and wisely declined.

The party were followed and harassed by the Indians, and narrowly escaped being slaughtered. Under cover of the darkness, the savages approached their camp, and from a ravine near by poured in a murderous volley upon them, and then resorted to their bows and arrows to prevent discovery. Strange to say, but two men were mortally wounded. The next day the party marched out, and in open field challenged the Indians for a fight, which they refused to accept. Seeing that the Crows were now openly hostile, and that to return by the same route was impossible, they started southward for the overland road, which point they reached after a most fatiguing and hazardous journey, with the loss of but three of their number, one of whom accidentally destroyed his own life.[1]

I will not attempt a description of my *personnel*, as, after a month's absence on a rusticating tour, for which I was but poorly prepared, on Monday evening, September 15th, at five o'clock, after a ride that day of more than forty miles, I rode into Bozeman, where I was refreshed by a cordial reunion with friends, who had begun to suspect that I was really lost in the mountains, or had been scalped by the Indians. But here I am at the close of my rambles, and at the end of a journey which, though not performed without some difficulties, taken all in all, is one of the most pleasant and profitable to mind and body that I ever made. It will ever constitute a bright spot in memory —an oasis in the journey of life—the remembrance of which is refreshing. In future years, when railroads shall checker this mountain country, and myriads of excited men and women shall come from every clime in splendid palace-cars to behold the curiosities of this wonderland of the world, I hope to be able to look back with pride to the day when I made the grand rounds on a cayuse pony, and recount to attentive listeners the wonderful events of one of the most remarkable journeys of a lifetime.

I hope, dear reader, that you have not grown weary in following the narrative of these protracted rambles; and I am sure that, if it should be your happy lot to go on such an excursion, you will acknowledge that the half has not been told, and will return with ample compensation for all the drenchings, tumbles in the mud, and other hardships encountered on a horseback-tour to the geysers.

[1] " Journal of Captain James Stuart, with Notes by S. T. Hauser," in " Contributions to the Historical Society," vol. i.

CHAPTER XVII.

Hitherto Obscurity of the Geyser Region.—The Cause —Legends.—Magic Cities.—Mysterious Inhabitants.—Jim Bridger.—Other Mountaineers visit this Region.—First Expedition.—Second.—Dr. Hayden's Expedition.—The National Park.—Its Variety of Wonders.—The grandest in the World.—Grand Exposition.

INCLOSED by a cordon of rugged, lofty mountain-ranges, which have been mentioned, it is not strange that the wonders of the Upper Yellowstone and Madison Basins have so long remained in comparative obscurity. All attempts to enter this region from the east and southeast were signal failures, the expeditions from the States heading this way being turned from their course to the southward by the insurmountable barriers, in the shape of the snowy glaciers of the Wind River range, throwing them out of reach of the Upper Yellowstone country; and the exploring-parties returning eastward from the Pacific slope, in their haste, seem to have avoided entering here, for fear, I suppose, of becoming "entangled" by the mountains on their homeward trip. Then, they had no positive information at that early day of the wonders that abound there. As it can be easily approached from the west, it remained for an expedition from this direction to explore and bring to light its hidden mysteries. This was not likely to take place until the "regions beyond" should be crowded with inhabitants, and energy and enterprise, stimulated by the floating legends, should spur them up to enter this dark corner of the earth.

Lewis and Clarke seem to have known nothing of this region, save of the "great lake" which is spread upon their chart, and of which they were doubtless informed by the Indians. The famous Jim Bridger, of Rocky Mountain notoriety, with one or two other white men, claim to have visited this enchanted land many years ago, and, from the rude descriptions which the former gave of it, it is probable that this is the same place he spoke of.

The legends and flying rumors that doubtless originated here, and have been circulated all over the West, colored by the superstitious imaginations of excited mountaineers and prospectors, compare favorably with the story of El Dorado, with its exhaustless treasures and golden cities, or the legends of the "Arabian Nights," with their magic cities and pearly palaces, that have excited the imaginations of so many youthful readers. Tradition told of a region where the trees were solid stone—of splendid palaces and gorgeous temples, with pearly gates, massive walls, gorgeous courts, and glittering, heaven-ascending spires. There were said to be mansions and lordly castles; but all of the inhabitants had, for some mortal sin, been turned to solid stone, and were still standing in their places as the grim, silent sentinels to guard the sacredness of the dreary solitude around the home of these fabulous beings. Curiously-wrought and strangely-colored specimens, brought down from these fairy regions by some venturesome explorer, were thought to be part of the war accoutrements and implements of a mysterious but doomed race of beings. Current stories of glittering diamonds and inexhaustible gold-fields tickled sensitive ears; while glowing accounts of burning plains, smoking furnaces, boiling caldrons, and noisy, rumbling, spouting springs, aroused the fears of many a superstitious red-man (they do not now like to enter this region, believing the evil spirit dwells here), and almost shook the faith of more than one "strong-minded" but astonished mountaineer.

It was thought at last, by all, that *something* wonderful must exist on the Upper Yellowstone, though just what it was no one knew; and, as the immense gold-seeking population moved into Montana, there came an increased desire to explore this mystic region. Bridger's statements could not be considered as myths, and the accounts of prospectors and trappers (some of whom I have talked with) who had been there, all seeming to harmonize, to a certain extent, were deemed worthy of credence.

But the first regularly-organized expedition that ventured to explore this region was fitted out in Montana, and went out in 1870. The reports of their explorations, by Mr. Langford, Lieutenant Doane, and others, through Eastern periodicals, were the first to bring the country into general notice. The way being fairly opened, Colonel Barlow led a Government expedition thither the following summer. Then in 1871 a large expedition, under Dr. Hayden, the United States Geologist, accompanied by a full corps of scientists, made extensive explorations, which were reported to the public the following year.

The concurrent testimony of all the explorers establishing the fact of the unfitness of this elevated mountain-region for agricultural or mining purposes, a bill was presented before, and passed by, Congress, setting apart this vast tract, sixty-five miles in length (east and west) by fifty-five in width, exempting it from settlement, and holding it as a reservation and "great national pleasure-ground" for our people. It is in the northwestern corner of Wyoming, and extends a few miles across the line into Montana. It embraces the sources of the great rivers before mentioned, the waters of which go forth from these mountain-sides to every point of the compass. It embraces, in part, that remarkable cluster of glacier-like peaks of the Wind River range, on the summit of one of which Bonneville went into such raptures many years ago; and also includes the Yellowstone Lake, Madison Lake, Mammoth Springs, the Great Falls and Cañon, Upper and Lower Geyser basins, together with all other intervening curiosities of this vast area. No person is permitted to settle or make improvements of any kind on it without permission from the proper authorities. When civilization advances sufficiently in the West, and visitors come in numbers to justify the building of hotels, and other improvements, such as making parks for the game, and preparing otherwise for the pleasure and entertainment of the tourist, this will be a wonderful resort for pleasure-seekers in the summer.

Although now shut out from the world, where it cannot be reached without a ride of four hundred miles on a rickety, rattling, jolting stage-coach, which is perfectly preposterous in the estimation of those in high life, who are unused to anything less than a Pullman palace-car or costly carriage, and a trip of a hundred miles or more, besides, over a moderately rough road, to be performed in a lumber wagon, with the remainder of the journey on the "hurricane-deck" of a cayuse (where the seas are sometimes rough), the very thought of which would cause an attack of spasmodic contraction of the nerves to timid souls, yet in no other spot of ground of the same compass is there grouped a greater variety of wonderful phenomena; and the time is coming when it will be the great central resort for the lovers of the grand, the wonderful, the beautiful, and the sublime in Nature, from all parts of the inhabited world.

Why, just think of it! The Mammoth Springs, with their wonderful architectural beauty, and the healing virtue of their waters, rival Saratoga and Long Branch—the famous watering-places of the Eastern States. The lovely cascade at Tower

Creek is not equaled by Minnehaha; while the Great Falls of the Yellowstone, with their symmetrical proportions containing "all the elements of picturesque beauty," and so intimately connected with all the strangely-fascinating enchantments of the delicately-carved and gorgeously-crowned Grand Cañon, excel in sublimity the world-known Niagara, or the soul-inspiring Yosemite. The view from Mount Washburn, or one of the glistening glaciers farther to the south, is equal to any of the Alpine views, which have inspired poets and stirred the souls of orators and artists in portraying their grandeur and beauty; while a visit to the charming solitudes along the pebbly strand of the crystal waters of Yellowstone Lake, with its emerald isles and weird surroundings, will cause every other like scene to fade into insignificance. Then comes the Upper Basin, once the centre of fiery volcanoes and powerful forces, where yet the earth is made to quake and tremble from the internal concussions and rumblings, as the stupendous volumes of steam and water are hurled upward from the superheated regions below.

It is conceded that no such cluster of wonders is exhibited elsewhere in the world. Let us imagine ourselves for once standing in a central position, where we can see every geyser in the basin. It is an extra occasion, and they are all out on parade, and all playing at once. There is good Old Faithful, always ready for her part, doing her best—the two-by-five-feet column playing to a height of one hundred and fifty feet—perfect in all the elements of geyser-action. Yonder the Beehive is sending up its graceful column two hundred feet heavenward, while the Giantess is just in the humor, and is making a gorgeous display of its—say—ten-feet volume to an altitude of two hundred and fifty feet. In the mean time the old Castle answers the summons, and, putting on its strength with alarming detonations, is belching forth a gigantic volume seventy feet above its crater; while over there, just above the Saw-mill, which is rallying all its force to the exhibition, rustling about and spurting upward its six-inch jet with as much self-importance as if it were the only geyser in the basin, we see the Grand, by a more than ordinary effort, overtopping all the rest with its heaven-ascending, graceful volume, three hundred feet in the air. Just below here the Riverside, the Comet, the complicated and fascinating Fantail, and the curiously-wrought Grotto, are all chiming in, and the grand old Giant, the chief of the basin, not to be left behind, or by any one outdone, is towering up with its six-feet fountain, swaying in the bright sunlight at an elevation of two hundred and fifty feet. In the mean time a hundred others of lesser note, we will say, are answering the call at this grand exposition, and coming out in all their native glory and surpassing beauty. Just listen to the terrible, awful rumblings and deafening thunders, as if the very earth would be moved from its foundation—the thousand reports of rushing waters and hissing steam, while Pluto is mustering all his forces, and Hades would feign disgorge itself and submerge our world. But then look upward at the immense masses of rising steam ascending higher and still higher, until lost in the heavens above; while every column is tinseled over with a robe of silver decked with all the prismatic colors, and every majestic fountain is encircled with a halo of gorgeous hues.

Who can, with pen or pencil, portray the terrific grandeur, and transcendent beauty and magnificence, of such a scene? With the fire and molten lava it would surpass Vesuvius or Etna; and here is water enough, if in close proximity, to rob either of them of half its fury and glory. Thus, almost right at home in our "own native land," in our own "Great West," we have attractions and wonders of which other countries might well be proud.

CHAPTER XVIII.

THRILLING ADVENTURES OF EXCURSIONISTS IN THE NATIONAL PARK: Nez-Percé Indians under Joseph.—Capture of Radersburg Party.—Bloody Work.—Mrs. Cowan, her Sister, and Brother, in Captivity.—Release of Captives.—Cowan's Miraculous Escape.—Radersburg Party attacked.—Kenck killed.—Escape of the Others.—Hardships endured.—Deitrich's Death.—Shiveley's Account of his Captivity.

IN time of peace there is no danger whatever of Indians in the National Park. They seem to have avoided it as much as possible in their travels; much less has it been their haunt or lurking-place. No place in the Rocky Mountains has been considered more secure from the ravages of hostile bands than this region of country, and tourists have always felt secure amid these solitudes. But during the present year (in August, 1877) the hostile Nez-Percés, under Joseph, on their march from Idaho toward the buffalo-country, while endeavoring to avoid the settlements of Montana, and pursued by the United States soldiers, were compelled to go through the park, entering at Henry's Lake, passing through Lower Geyser Basin, crossing the Yellowstone River, near Muddy Geyser, and going out through a pass at the head of Clark's Fork.

The adventures of the parties of tourists who were intercepted by the Nez-Percés while making the grand rounds, the killing of several of them, the wounding of others, and the trials and hardships encountered by those who made good their escape, are matters of such thrilling interest to the public throughout the entire country, that I have thought it proper to give an account of them in these pages. I have talked with many of the participants in the tragic scenes here described, and the following is substantially correct :

The Radersburg party, consisting of George F. Cowan and wife, and Charles Mann, of Radersburg; Miss Ida Carpenter and Mr. Meyers, of Missouri Valley ; William Dingee, Albert Oldham, and Frank Carpenter, of Helena, left Radersburg on Monday, the 6th of August, for the National Park. They went by way of Sterling and up the Madison River to the Lower Geyser Basin, traveling by wagon and carriage. Here they made their permanent camp, and left their vehicles, making the rest of the tour through Wonderland on horseback. They visited the Upper Geyser Basin, and three members of the party visited also the Yellowstone Falls and the lake. It was as cheerful a party as ever went through the park. They lived well, passed the evenings around the camp-fire listening to music from guitar and violin, little dreaming that a savage foe was approaching so near them. On the night of the 23d, having returned to their camp, they prepared to start homeward the following day. About five o'clock next morning, while Arnold and Dingee (the only persons up in camp) were making the camp-fire, three Indians were discovered approaching. They came up and alighted from their horses. The party were all up in short order and questioned the Indians, who, after some prevarications, stated that they were Nez-Percés under Looking-Glass, that Looking-Glass was the friend of the white man, " would not hurt white man, but would fight soldiers," and that his band of two hundred warriors were in camp a short distance below, in the timber. Many Indians could now be seen, and the party, after consulting with each other, as they had no adequate means of defense, concluded to move out of camp down the Firehole River toward home. They were encouraged to take this course from the fact that one of the Indians assured them that they need apprehend no danger, as they were friends to the white man, and he would himself escort the party safely through the entire Indian camp, when they could go on their journey homeward. This also confirmed what the party had heard before coming to the park, namely, that the Nez-Percés were permitted by the authorities to pass through the Territory to the Yellowstone without molestation. The party then harnessed and saddled their horses, and proceeded homeward, without waiting to prepare breakfast. They were, however, soon surrounded by a large party of warriors, who told them that it would not be safe for them to travel on that road, as there were bad Indians behind who would kill all of the party if they met them. They then told the tourists that their only safe plan would be to turn back and go with them; that they would protect them, and the bad Indians should not hurt them; and that they would conduct the party to a place from which they could soon reach the white settlements.

While they were consulting what course to pursue, the Indians, who were all well armed, and some with their guns unslung and ready for instant use, compelled the party to turn round and fall into their line of march.

After traveling for about two miles up the east fork of Firehole River, the wagon and carriage had to be abandoned on account of the fallen timber, over which they could not pass. The horses were unhitched and saddled for Mrs. Cowan and her sister Ida to ride upon. While the boys were saddling up, Mr. Frank Carpenter said he would go to the front, find Looking-Glass, and see if he would not let them go on home, and for six needle-gun cartridges hired an Indian to conduct him thither. He found the chief eight miles farther on, at the foot of a steep mountain, just west of Mary's Lake, where the Indians had camped for noon. He shook hands with Looking-Glass, and asked him if he was a friend, to which he responded: "Yes—no kill citizens."

While Mr. Cowan was telling him of the party, up came White Bird (who is also a chief of some note among the Nez-Percés), accompanied by Shively, who had been captured the evening before, and was forced to act as guide for the Indians. White Bird invited him to his lodge, where Frank was plied with questions as to who they were, where they were from, where they were going, etc. He gave the chief full particulars, and asked him if they could not go home. He said:

"Yes; no kill citizens, but kill Lewiston soldiers all time—heap kill."

In the mean time the Indians had hurried their captives forward till they came to White Bird's camp. This dignitary informed them that they could return home, but that he would be under the necessity of taking their horses, arms, and ammunition. He told them that he would give them other horses to ride upon, and other guns with three cartridges each in place of those taken from them. This he did, according to his word. At this juncture the chiefs ordered camp to be broken, and the march resumed. The captives were commanded to depart on the back trail, which order was obeyed without hesitation by the little party, who were, however, filled with dread, as they saw that they were followed by forty or fifty savages, the most ferocious-looking in the camp, whose dark, snake-like eyes were fixed upon them with murderous intent, and who, after White Bird confessing that he could not longer control them, had gone forward, and now became insolent, taking their guns, blankets, and other property, and making the woods resound with their hideous yells. About this time Dingee and Arnold dodged into the brush and made their escape. The party were dogged by the bloodthirsty fiends for a short distance farther, when they were again ordered to halt, and then to turn round and go back the other way. It was now evident that the savages meant mischief, the object of this marching and counter-marching being only to let the other chiefs get out of the way. The warriors then took the captives back to a place not far from where White Bird had left them, where the trail ascends a little knoll, near the thick timber at the foot of the mountain, where they began their bloody work.

Cowan and his wife were riding in advance, when two Indians came dashing down the hill in front of them. The savages halted, and one of them raised his rifle and fired, the ball passing through Cowan's right thigh. He slipped from his horse, and being unable to use his wounded leg, fell to the ground. Instantly his wife was at his side bending over him, when presently two Indians came up, one of whom raised his revolver and pointed it at Cowan's head, intending to finish the bloody deed. Mrs. Cowan, seeing this, threw her arms around her husband's neck and her body in front of his face to shield him from the deadly missile, and implored the Indian to take her life first. He replied, "No, me kill old ones first," and seized her right hand to drag her from her husband; but she still clung with heroic strength to his neck with the other hand. This gave the other Indian a fair view of Cowan's head, and he instantly drew his revolver and fired, the ball taking effect just above the left temple, when the unfortunate man was left for dead. When the firing commenced the party scattered, and several of them succeeded in escaping to the brush. Albert Oldham was shot through the face, the ball passing through his tongue, but inflicting no serious injury. He fell near the timber, and was left for dead, though he succeeded in making his escape, and after four days and five nights, in the wilderness without food or shelter, suffering intensely from cold, hunger, and loss of blood, was picked up by Howard's command. Charles Mann reached the timber with a bullet-hole through his hat, the ball just grazing the scalp, and was taken in by some Bannack scouts, and returned with Howard to look after the rest of the party, who were supposed to be dead. Meyers, though suffering severely with a scalded foot, outran the Indians a fair race for several miles and joined the soldiers. Dingee and Arnold, who got away from the party before the firing commenced, after spending five days and nights in the mountains without food, fire, or coats upon their backs, when almost despairing, joined the command near Henry's Lake.

While the firing was going on, Frank Carpenter saw a young chief who had him in charge, with his gun cocked and aimed directly at his breast. He thought his time had come, and, remembering that these Indians are Catholics, he made the sign of the cross, when the Indian threw up his gun and said, "Come quick, me no kill—me save you!" Carpenter then ran to where his sister was bending over her husband (this was before Cowan was shot in the head) to try to assist them, when the chief ordered him away, and placed him behind some brush, telling him to keep still. He asked the Indian to spare the white girls, and he said he would.

After the firing was over, Mrs. Cowan was torn away from her husband, who was thought to be lifeless, as his head had been pounded with stones by these fiends in human form, and whose life she had labored so hard to save, really endangering her own in the heroic effort. She and her sister were each lashed on a horse behind a savage, and with their brother, who had been spared, were led into captivity, and started eastward on the trail. But I will permit Mr. Carpenter to relate the story of the captivity and release of himself and sister, as told by him to the author, and also published in the Helena papers. He says:

"Finally, after what seemed an age to me, we moved out of the brush and commenced driving horses up the hill. Going along the trail about two miles, I first saw my sister, Mrs. Cowan. In reply to my inquiries she said that Ida, the last she saw of her, was on a horse behind an Indian, and that she thought the rest of the party were all killed. We then got separated on different trails, and did not see each other until we met in camp, about ten o'clock at night.

"We slept none that night. Emma said she saw Albert Oldham shot and fall from his horse. Cowan was first shot through the leg. She ran to him. An Indian came up, placed a pistol near their heads, fired, and George fell, with her arms around his neck. The Indian dragged her away, and as she was being put on a horse she looked back and saw Cowan place his hand to his head. She saw an Indian throw a big rock on Cowan's head, crushing it as she thinks. She recollects no more until seeing me, and finding herself on a horse behind an Indian.

"The next morning I was told that I was to be killed, and that my sisters were to be put on pack-animals and turned loose. I asked White Bird to keep the girls until they came to some settlement or road, for they would get lost in the park and perish if alone. The camp began to move, and my chief told me to travel with his squaw, as he was going to hunt elk. About noon we crossed the Yellowstone, nearly opposite the Muddy Geyser. I there saw my sister Ida for the first time. She ran toward me, but I told her to go back, that I would come to her as soon as I could. A cry of 'Soldiers!' was raised, and the warriors recrossed the river on a run, and we saw no more of them. About a dozen remained with the camp. After dinner Emma, Ida, and Shively, came over where I was, to have a talk.

" Later in the afternoon White Bird called a council of the chiefs present, to decide what should be done with us. In the council were White Bird, a Snake chief named Little Bear, a Crow chief, the chief who claimed me, and two young chiefs. White Bird spoke in our behalf for about thirty minutes, his main argument being that if they killed us the citizens of Montana would retaliate by killing the Nez-Percés. Little Bear got up and talked a long time. He pawed the ground and gesticulated fiercely. He wanted to kill me and keep my sister for his squaw—as an Indian afterward told me.

" White Bird lit a pipe, took a few puffs, and passed it round the circle. Those who smoked were in favor of letting us go. I watched them—oh, how eagerly! Never in my life did I experience such delight in seeing a person smoke! Twice the pipe passed around the circle. *Four of the chiefs smoked the pipe, and three refused.*

" The council dispersed. White Bird informed me that myself and sisters should go home. He brought two horses for my sisters to ride, intimating that I could walk, and I replied that all I wanted was a chance. Mrs. Cowan's riding-habit was brought to her; she and Ida were mounted. White Bird escorted us about a mile. He then said: 'Go home—go quick! You no meet Indians on trail—they gone back to Henry's Lake to fight Lewiston soldiers. I no want to fight Montana citizens or soldiers. You tell Bozeman people, Montana people, if Montana soldiers fight us any more, we kill all white women, papooses, citizens—everybody. We kill all—no let them go!

We go to Shoshone country. You get to Bozeman in three days. Good-by.'

"If White Bird had seen us make time for the next three miles he would have had sufficient evidence that we were obeying his advice to 'go quick.' But darkness overtook us when we had gone some four or five miles. We went up the timber, about two miles southwest of Sulphur Mountain, crept into some underbrush, and passed the night the best we could. My sisters suffered from cold, they having got their dresses pretty wet in swimming the Yellowstone. Sunday morning we struck across the country, toward Bozeman, keeping in the timber until we struck the trail going down to the falls, and we came out within half a mile of where we afterward learned the Helena party were camped. If I had known it, I could have warned them, and the lives of Kenck and Deitrich would have been saved. Twelve miles from the springs we met Lieutenant Schofield and party. They showed us every possible attention.

"Twenty minutes later we saw Pfister coming down the trail, who informed us of the attack on the Helena party that day noon. Lieutenant Schofield escorted us to the springs, where we arrived at 10 P. M. Monday we continued on to Bottler's ranch, where we met many kind friends. On Tuesday we arrived at Bozeman, having been met on the road by Mr. David Boreum with carriages."

But, to return to Mr. Cowan. It was reported that he was shot through the head, and no one entertained the hope that he was alive. But it seems that he was not born to be killed by an Indian bullet. The ball *flattened*, and did not enter the skull. Mr. Cowan thinks he remained insensible about two hours—from three o'clock (at which time the shooting took place) till five, when he regained his consciousness. At first, he hardly knew whether he was in this world or some other, as he remembered seeing the Indian aim directly at his head, and experienced a sensation as if the ball had gone crashing through his brain. I suppose he thought he was surely killed. But, on opening his eyes, he recognized the place, and was sure that he was still on Mother Earth, though he had been dragged (as he supposed) some distance from the place where he fell. His first impulse was to feel for his hair, which he found all right, except that it was clotted with blood from the bullet-wound and the gashes made by the stones with which he was pounded. Finding that his wounds were not necessarily fatal, and thinking himself entirely alone, he drew himself up by the boughs of a tree, and was standing on his feet, when he discovered an Indian approaching him with rifle in hand ready for use, twenty yards away. Thinking to escape from the Indian, Mr. Cowan started toward a clump of bushes not far away, and, while looking back over his shoulder to see how close the savage was upon him, the Indian fired, the ball striking Cowan on the point of the left hip and coming out in front of the abdomen. He fell on his face in some high grass, about twenty yards from the trail, where he remained perfectly still, thinking his case hopeless now, and every moment expecting the Indian to come up and complete his work. But he never came. About twenty minutes elapsed, when a party of hostiles passed along the trail, but did not discover the wounded man. Mr. Cowan kept his place for half an hour after these Indians passed, and, everything being silent as death (it was now dark), he cautiously surveyed the position, and, finding himself alone, he took another inventory of his injuries, the result of which gave him some hope. Finding himself unable to stand upon his feet, he commenced to crawl, desiring to get to a place of greater safety, which he kept up till midnight, when he lay down and wished for day.

Mr. Cowan's condition at this time would appear anything but hopeful. With three severe wounds on his person, suffering from intense cold, hunger, and loss of blood, in a vast wilderness inhabited by wild beasts and (at this time) savage men, unable to stand upon his feet, and almost distracted at the thought that his wife was murdered or led away into a cruel bondage, his condition excites the liveliest sympathy. But he was not the man to give up. He remembered that some of the party had carelessly dropped a few matches and spilt a small quantity of parched coffee at the camp in Firehole Basin; also, that an empty can had been left there. If the matches could be secured and the coffee and can could be found, he would have fire and get some nourishment which would sustain life, possibly, till he could be rescued. The old camp was twelve miles away; but, nothing daunted, Mr. Cowan started on the perilous journey. On his way, passing near the abandoned wagons, he crawled to them in the vain hope of getting something in the shape of clothing to keep him warm. Here he found his bird-dog keeping faithful watch and patiently waiting for its master's return. The dog was delighted to see him, seemed to show great sympathy for him in his afflictions, and attended him in all of his after-travels. Finally, after crawling on his hands and knees for four days and nights, through dense timber and brush, resting at intervals, on Tuesday evening Mr. Cowan reached the camp where they were captured, where he found the matches and coffee-grains scattered in the dirt. He now felt safe, as he had fire to warm him, coffee to drink, and a dog that he could kill and eat, if necessity required.

The next day (Wednesday), just before noon, he was found by two of General Howard's scouts, and the following day the advance-guard came up, with whom was Mr. Arnold, who brought Cowan the first intelligence of the safety of his wife.

Mr. Cowan was placed in a wagon, and taken with the command to the Yellowstone, from which place, accompanied by Arnold, who was untiring in his efforts to minister to the wants of his friend, he was sent to Bozeman, where, meeting his wife on the way, and, after several other hair-breadth escapes, he arrived in safety, and received the congratulations of a host of friends who had given him up for dead. What a joyful occasion, as husband and wife met again, after such a long and painful separation!

The Helena party was composed of the following persons: A. J. Weikert, Frederick Pfister, Richard Deitrich, Joseph Roberts, Charles Kenck, Jack Stewart, August Foller, Leslie Wilkie, L. Duncan, and Benjamin Stone (colored cook).

On the morning of the 25th of August the tourists started from the Yellowstone Falls, expecting to encamp that night at the Mud Geysers, about nine or ten miles distant, but, on reaching Sulphur Mountain, and riding to the summit, they discovered a moving body several miles ahead, which was first pronounced a band of elk, then a large party of tourists, but which it was soon ascertained was a troop of Indians. The tourists soon discovered the main Indian camp on the east bank of the Yellowstone. The entire party at once returned to within three miles of the falls, rode one mile from the trail west, through the timber, and went into camp in a little opening near a stream that puts into the Yellowstone. They were not disturbed during the night. No one knew what tribe the Indians which they had met belonged to. Next morning, Weikert and Wilkie volunteered to act as scouts, with the understanding that if danger threatened they were to fire their guns, which should be the signal for the party to escape for their lives.

About eleven o'clock the cook was preparing dinner, and most of the boys were lying asleep or lounging about camp, when the party were startled by the crack of a gun, and immediately a full volley was fired into the camp by a band of savages not thirty yards away, who rushed forward, firing as they came, and making the woods ring with their savage war-whoop. Kenck was killed instantly, and Stewart received a severe wound in the hip, but succeeded in getting away. The rest of the party scattered and ran for the woods, followed by showers of bullets, and succeeded in making their escape.

The scouts had failed to discover Indians on account of the haze, and were returning. When about two miles from camp they discovered the savages in ambush for them, and wheeled their horses to retreat. The Indians fired, hitting Weikert in the shoulder, while another bullet carried away the stock of his rifle, and bullets were whizzing thickly around their heads like hailstones. The boys escaped from the Indians and galloped to a place near the camp and fired two shots —the signal agreed upon. No response came. With throbbing hearts they shouted the names of their party, but could only hear the echo of their own voices in return. Determined to know the worst, the brave boys went into camp, where the broken shot-guns, provisions, and camp-equipage piled on the smouldering camp-fire, told the fearful tale. With sad hearts they started homeward. They soon came up with Stewart and Stone. Stewart was badly wounded, and Stone was helping him along. Both were exhausted. The noble-hearted scouts gave up their horses to their helpless comrades and trudged onward the long, weary night without complaint, reaching the Mammoth Springs next morning, having traveled forty-five miles since the attack. Here they met Carpenter and his sisters, who had just arrived, and during the day all the survivors of the Helena party arrived except Roberts and Foller. These boys—one scarcely twenty and the other seventeen years of age—succeeded in reaching the timber amid a shower of deadly missiles, and started in a northwesterly direction across the mountains through the forest, hoping thus to avoid the Indians, who they supposed would follow them.

Lost amid the dreary solitudes of these mountains without compass or guide, destitute of food or sufficient raiment to keep them warm, their feet sore and bleeding, it is a wonder that they should escape so well. Of their experience Roberts says:

"Foller and I traveled from about noon until dark—direction west, hugging the timbered mountain-side. We lay down supperless to sleep. Foller, better off than I, had a coat, so I took the inside next a big log, with Foller as outside layer. We were up at daybreak next morning, and continued our tramp. We turned a little north of west, aiming to strike the Madison River. Had nothing to eat during the day except some berries plucked from bushes along the way. Water we found in sloughs and springs. Still following the side and ridge of mountains we bivouacked at dark in the manner of the night before.

"On the morning of the 28th, about nine o'clock, we struck the summit of the divide separating the waters of the Madison and Yellowstone. Starting down a dry gulch, we followed it until we struck a small stream, which led us to the river. Traveling down the Madison some miles we found a vacant cabin. We felt encouraged to rest here a bit, and ease our blistered feet. Foller, having a tackle, tried his luck at angling, and caught three fish. These we roasted, having made a fire; ate two of the fish, and saved the third for emergencies. Resumed our march down-stream, making our bed that night in tall grass near the river.

"Rose early on the morning of the 29th and resumed our

march. Traveled some miles, and then sat down and breakfasted on part of the remaining fish. About noon, on turning a bend, we saw several men on the opposite side of the river, and hailed them. They proved to be a party with wagons transporting supplies to General Howard's command, then at Henry's Lake. One of them mounted and forded the river, leading two animals to convey us over. The party took good care of us— gave us first a small dram of whiskey and then carefully rationed us. Afterward, providing us with canned salmon, tomatoes, hard-tack, a loaf of bread, etc., they gave us the direction to Virginia City, and we proceeded on, still afoot, until night, when we camped in a deserted house.

"Traveling until noon of the 30th, we fell in with a man looking for stock. He sent us to his wagon, while he went off after stray horses. When he returned we bargained with him to take us to Virginia, where we arrived safely the same evening."

On Saturday, September 1st, Weikert and McCartney had returned to the place of attack in search of the missing, to bury them if dead, and bring them in if wounded; while Deitrich, a man by the name of Stoner, and Stone (colored), remained at the springs to assist in caring for the wounded when they should arrive. All the rest had left and gone toward Bozeman. A party of Indians made their appearance and commenced firing. Stoner and Stone succeeded in getting safely to Doane's camp just below, but Deitrich was killed. Weikert and McCartney, after burying Kenck's body, were returning to the springs, when they were attacked by the same party of Indians, and had a narrow escape, one of the scouts having his horse shot under him.

It is quite amusing to hear Ben Stone (the colored cook) relate the story of his adventures. The reporter asked: "What did you do, Ben, when the Indians commenced firing into the camp on the Yellowstone?"

"Why, sah, I jes run as fast as my legs could carry me; and dat was mighty fast, I tell you, when de bullets war a-whizzin' 'round me like bees in June. I struck for de timber where dar was no Injuns, if dat place war to be found. But de whole woods 'peared to be full ob 'em from de way de bullets flew. Soon as I got out o' sight—and it wasn't long, I tell you—de all-important question was to find a place to hide, so dey wouldn't find me if dey follered us. Dis now become de all-absorbin' topic, and dar was no time to lose. Whar could I go? I wanted to git in a place dat was de same color ob myself, you see. I come to a big mud-hole and I saw it was black, and I knowed I was black—jes de same color, you see. Says I to myself, 'Dey won't see me in heah.' So I jumped right into de middle ob it, and jes stuck my nose out to get bref—a very important item, you know—and dar I laid in dat mud-hole till de last red rascal was gone."

In speaking of the attack at Mammoth Springs, Ben said he was preparing some refreshments for the wounded who should come with Weikert and McCartney, when, on looking out, he saw an Indian peeping from behind the rocks, and then he remarked to himself, "Mr. Stone, it is about time you war gettin' out o' heah."

He continued: "I den struck for tall timber wid all my might, an' what do you think, sah? Why, I looked ahead, and dar I saw a red-skin a-comin' right toward me as fast as he could ride. We war a-comin' right meetin' each oder, but I didn't want to cultivate no sich 'quaintances den. So I said to myself: 'Dis won't neber do, Ben; you must take anudder trail;' an' I wasn't long a-decidin' de p'int, neider. I lit out; de Injun saw me, and heah he come right after me. I thought I was a gone darkey den, an' no mistake about it."

"How in the world did you get away from him, Ben?"

"Why, sah, jes' by clean runnin'. You see, I run ober a little ridge, an' war out o' sight ob de Injun foh jus' half a minit. Dar war a little pine-tree a-standin' right in de trail. Somethin' 'peared to say to me, 'Ben, you better clime de tree.' I jes' put my hands on a limb dat stuck out, an' was up in de branches in no time. I hadn't mor'n got in de tree till dat sneakin' rascal came along my trail an' stopped right under me. He put his hand up to his ear, leant forred, as if he was a-lis'nin' for somethin'—an' he was. It was me he was a-huntin', an' I thought my time had come. Why, sah, if you b'leeve me, I could jis a-put my foot right on top o' his head, he war so close. *But I didn't do it.* No, sah, not me! It warn't no time foh playin' jokes."

"What did you do, Ben?"

"Why, bless your soul, what could I do but stan' dar an' hug dat tree and hol' my bref, so as he wouldn't heah me, till he went on to look foh me behind some rocks at anudder place?"

The Indian never dreamed of looking up in the tree for his prey, and it was luck for Ben that he did not. Stone camped among the branches of the friendly pine till near evening. He then came down and started up the mountain-side toward the thick timber, crawling on his hands and knees for fear of being discovered.

"What did you think, about this time, Mr. Stone?"

"I thought, sah, if I had been on my knees mo' foh de las' twenty yeahs, it would hav' bin better foh dis chile."

"Did you pray any, Ben?"

"Pray? Well, I jes' guess I did. If I eber prayed in my life, it was den an' dar. I thought of all de meanness I had eber done in all my life—an' it was a heap, too. I said to myself,

'Dis is five times since I been in dese mountains dat de ole fellow called foh me, an' five times he let me go agin; and now, if he'll only let me go dis one time mo', I won't swear no mo', I won't drink no mo' whiskey, nor I won't play no mo' cards long as I lib—so I won't. De Lor' bress your soul, sah, it war enuff to make de biggest sinner in de worl' pray, to hab dem cussed Injuns a-huntin' him down to take his scalp!"

But I fear that our hero forgot his prayer and the vows he made, from the language he used and the smell of his breath when he related this story.

But Ben's troubles were not yet at an end. He says: "I kep' a crawlin' an' a crawlin', neber feelin' safe, till I got away up in de woods, when what should I meet but a great rousin' big grizzly bar! It was a-comin' right down de trail toward me. What was I to do now? Dar de Injuns war on one side an' de bar on de oder, an' I was between 'em.' Peared like dey war in cahort, and war a-goin' to hab me anyhow. Said I to myself: 'Mr. Stone, you is in a tight place agin. Which'll you take, de Injuns or de bar?' an' says I, 'I've tried de Injuns, an' don't want no mo' to do wid em—*I'll take de bar.*'"

Ben thought that time brings strange bedfellows. Bruin sat up on his haunches and grinned awhile at his newly-found companion, then turned away in disgust, and left him alone in his glory.

While on the hill, Stone heard several shots fired, and remarked: "Dat was for Weikart an' dat for McCartney. Ah, boys, you is in bad hands now, but I can't help you none! I'se got no gun, and you'll jes' have to fight it out or save yo'selves like I did—by clean runnin'—which, after all, in my 'pinyun, am de best an' safest way to fight Injuns."

Ben secreted himself in the thick timber, where he remained until the next day.

In the afternoon he sallied out, and soon after heard the tinkling of bells. "Joseph's camp," muttered he; "de tarnal camp, it 'pears to be eb'rywhar! I mus' steer 'round it." He crawled a few steps farther, when he was accosted in stentorian tones by—

"Who goes there?"

"Ben Stone, sah!" answered our hero.

"Come forward, Ben Stone," responded the voice.

"I'se a comin'," answered Ben, as he promptly obeyed the summons.

When Ben came into camp, a man of swarthy complexion, and dressed in buckskin, came up, shook hands with him, and said, "We have had scouts out searching for you all day."

An Indian also came up, reached out his hand, and said, "How!"

"You is a goner, shuah, dis time," remarked the colored man to himself once more. "Dat was Joseph hisself dat shook hands wid me, an' I hab walked right into de lion's mouf."

And they could not persuade him that it was not the Nez-Percé camp until Weikert returned and told him that it was Lieutenant Doane with his Crow scouts.

Reference has been made to Shively. He was on his way from the Black Hills, had stopped to see the geysers, and was just waiting for the Radersburg party to complete their tour of observation, expecting to travel in company with them to the settlements, when he was captured by the Nez-Percés on the evening of the 23d of August, and compelled to act as guide for them. His story is thrilling, and I will permit him to relate it himself, as gathered from the Territorial papers. He says, in substance:

"On the evening of the second day, after leaving the Radersburg party, I was camped in the Lower Geyser Basin. I was eating my supper, and, on hearing a slight noise, looked up, and, to my astonishment, four Indians, in war-paint, were standing within ten feet of me, and twenty or thirty more had surrounded me not more than forty feet off. I sprang for my gun, but was rudely pushed back. I then asked them what Indians they were, and they answered 'Sioux.' I said, 'No.' Then one of them said, 'Nez-Percés.' They then commenced to gesticulate wildly, and a loud conversation was kept up between them. I thought the exhibition of a little bravery might help me, so I folded my arms and told them to shoot, that I was not afraid to die. A brother of Looking-Glass then came up, placed his hand on my heart, and held it there a minute or two, and exclaimed, 'Hyas, skookum-tum-tum!' meaning 'strong heart' in Chinook. He then said in English, 'Come with me,' walked a few steps, told me to get on a pony that he pointed out, jumped up behind me, and all started for the main camp, a short distance below. While this was taking place, the other Indians had taken my gun, blankets, horses—in fact, everything I had. Arriving at the main camp, a council of the chiefs was formed, and I was told to take a seat inside the circle. They asked me who I was, and what I was doing there. I told them. They asked me if I would show them the best trail leading out of the park to Wind River, where they were going. I told them I would, as I knew all about the country. This seemed to be satisfactory, and the council broke up, and the camp moved up a mile or two, where an encampment for the night was formed. A robe was given me, and an Indian named Joe was detailed to sleep with me. He spoke very good English; said that I must not attempt to escape; that he would be my friend; that they had come that way to get away from Howard; that the trail by that route to Wind River was not known to them, but other Indians had told them about it, and that if I told them the truth they would not harm me. As I could not help myself, I promised all they asked, and kept my promise. All the time I was with them, I always showed a willingness to get on or off a horse when they told me; and, if an Indian rode behind me on the horse, I offered no objections, and to this fact I am probably indebted for kind treatment. After breaking camp the next morning, I was ordered to mount. An Indian mounted behind, and I was started ahead with mounted and armed Indians on each side and behind me. While camped the next day, about noon, the Radersburg party were brought into camp. Shortly afterward, a march was made toward Yellowstone Lake, I still being kept some distance in the advance. After traveling about a mile, I heard seven distinct shots fired, and supposed all the persons had been killed, but that evening Joe told me that only two men had been shot, and the next morning I saw Mrs. Cowan and Miss Carpenter, and was allowed to speak to them, and we traveled near together all that day. Through this terrible ordeal, the sisters behaved nobly and with the utmost fortitude, although Mrs. Cowan's mental agony at thought of her husband wounded, and perhaps dead, and they three in the hands of savages, was enough to have driven her distracted. With all their savagery and ferocity, let it be said and remembered to the credit of the Nez-Percés, that these ladies were treated with all respect, and protected from all harm, while their prisoners.

"The next day, Frank Carpenter and his sisters were permitted to go, and the Indians moved to the Yellowstone, and from there moved over to the head-waters, or rather a tributary, of Clark's fork. The first night of our arrival being quite dark, I slipped out of camp and started for the Mammoth Hot Springs, which I reached after traveling two whole nights and one day. Here I found no one, but did find some potatoes already cooked, which greatly revived me after my long fast—having had nothing to eat from the time of leaving the Indian camp. I then started for Henderson's ranch, which I found destroyed, but plenty of provisions lying around. I got some eggs, and, while cooking them, Mr. J. W. Schuler, of Butte City, who was returning from the Clark's Fork mines, rode up. He kindly gave me his horse to ride, he going on foot. That night, early, we reached Dailey's ranch, where we received the kindest treatment, and Mr. Dailey loaned me a horse on which to ride to Bozeman.

"I was with the Indians thirteen days, and was treated very well all the time. They traveled very leisurely, not averaging, for the whole time, more than five miles a day. Joe said they were not afraid of Howard. He also said that they did not intend to return to Idaho, as the agent there, John Hall, was a bad man, and would not give them what was due them; that they would remain somewhere in the Big Horn country, and, if the soldiers came, they would join in with the Sioux and Crows and whip them."

Thus ends the brief recital of some of the most startling incidents of Western adventure that it has ever been the lot of the historian to chronicle. Imagine the gloom that was cast over the entire Territory of Montana when the report of these tragic events was first flashed over the wires, and whispered by quivering lips and with throbbing hearts from one to another throughout the gorges and glens of the Rocky Mountains! Among the victims was some of the best blood of our Territory. It was thought that all had fallen under the bloody scalping-knife, or were led away into captivity. Many homes and hearts were made desolate. It turned out that but two of the party were killed. They were worthy citizens of Helena, and their loss is deeply deplored by all. But many hearts were raised in grateful remembrance to the Father of Mercies that so many were spared. Their deliverance was almost miraculous.

Many incidents are related which, for want of space, cannot be recorded here, but enough has been recited to show that the heroic age has not yet passed. The undaunted courage and devotion of Mrs. Cowan in saving her husband's life (for she did save it), the fortitude of herself and younger sister, as shown when in the hands of their captors, the endurance of Cowan and his fellow-sufferers, the bravery of Shively, and the courage and friendship of Arnold, Weikert, and others, in caring for their unfortunate companions, will be remembered, rehearsed, and admired, by all lovers of such noble traits of character wherever they are known, as long as those grand old mountains stand as silent witnesses, but perpetual reminders, of the scenes here related.

DIRECTIONS FOR TOURISTS
CONCERNING ROUTES, DISTANCES, OUTFITS, EXPENSES, WITH OTHER USEFUL INFORMATION ABOUT THE YELLOWSTONE PARK.

PREFATORY.

WHEN "Rambles in Wonderland" was first published, it was not intended for a guide-book, but merely an account of what was considered the most wonderful trip of a life-time, and a description of the principal objects of interest on the route. Since that time many important changes have taken place. Two great lines of railroad have been built, one almost and the other quite to the border of the Park. Besides this, new curiosities have been discovered, wagon-roads made, stage-lines established, new trails opened up, and hotels and other accommodations provided which have greatly lessened the labor and expense, and added to the convenience of the thousands of pleasure-seekers that are annually flocking to this wonderland of the world.

The general favor with which the aboved-named book has been received by the public—for which the author is very grateful—and a desire to contribute something more to the interest and general welfare of those who contemplate making a tour to the Yellowstone National Park, has prompted the preparation of the following pages, which contain many items of information relative to routes, outfits, expenses, etc., that will prove valuable to tourists.

LOCATION, AREA, AND HISTORY OF THE PARK

The Yellowstone National Park is in the north-western corner of Wyoming, extends a few miles northward into Montana, and takes a small corner of Eastern Idaho. It is, according to P. W. Norris, sixty-two miles in length from north to south, and fifty-four miles in width from east to west, embracing an area of three thousand three hundred and forty-eight square miles. The action of Congress setting it apart as a national pleasure-ground was based principally upon the report of Dr. F. V. Hayden, United States Geologist in 1871. (See Rambles, page 154.) The bill was introduced into the Senate in December of that year, by S. C. Pomeroy, of Kansas; and about the same time a similar bill was presented before the House by Hon. William H. Claggett, then Delegate from Montana. The bill had able advocates in both Houses, passed with little or no opposition, and became a law March 1, 1872. It was a happy conception, and the Park constitutes one of the grandest gifts of a nation to its citizens. The following is a copy of the bill:

Be it enacted, by the Senate and House of Representatives of the United States of America in Congress assembled, That the tract of land in the Territories of Montana and Wyoming, lying near the head-waters of the Yellowstone River, and described as follows—to wit: Commencing at the junction of Gardiner's River with the Yellowstone River and running east to the meridian passing ten miles to the eastward of the most eastern point of Yellowstone Lake; thence south along the said meridian to the parallel of latitude passing ten miles south of the most southern point of Yellowstone Lake; thence west along said parallel to the meridian passing fifteen miles west of the most western point of Madison Lake; thence north along said meridian to the latitude of the junction of the Yellowstone and Gardiner's rivers; thence east to the place of beginning—is hereby reserved and withdrawn from settlement, occupancy, or sale under the laws of the United States, and dedicated and set apart as a public park, or pleasure-ground, for the benefit and enjoyment of the people; and all persons who shall locate, settle upon, or occupy the same or any part thereof, except as hereinafter provided, shall be considered trespassers and removed therefrom.

Sec. 2. That said public park shall be under the exclusive control of the Secretary of the Interior, whose duty it shall be, as soon as practicable, to make and publish such rules and regulations as he may deem necessary or proper for the care and management of the same. Such regulations shall provide for the preservation from injury or spoliation of all timber, mineral deposits, natural curiosities or wonders within said Park, and their retention in their natural condition.

The Secretary may, in his discretion, grant leases for building purposes, for terms not exceeding ten years, of small parcels of ground, at such places in said Park as shall require the erection of buildings for the accommodation of visitors; all of the proceeds of said leases, and all other revenues that may be derived from any source connected with said Park, to be expended, under his direction, in the management of the same, and the construction of roads and bridle-paths therein. He shall provide against the wanton destruction of the fish and game found within said Park, and against their capture or destruction for the purpose of merchandise or profit. He shall also cause all persons trespassing upon the same after the passage of this act to be removed therefrom, and generally shall be authorized to take all such measures as shall be necessary or proper to fully carry out the objects and purposes of this act.

The Yellowstone Park does not consist simply of one park, or basin, but is made up of many smaller basins, parks, and valleys, which are cut through in places by deep cañons and rugged water-courses, and separated by mountain ranges which are generally covered with pine forests and studded with bristling peaks that rear their snow-clad summits from eight thousand to twelve thousand feet above the level of the sea.

It is supposed by many that a man by the name of Colter, who was honorably discharged from Lewis and Clarke's expedition, visited this region some time about 1806-10. If so, he is probably the first white man who ever beheld its wonders. That trappers visited it in very early times is evident from the remains of a cabin and other relics discovered by Col. Norris near the Grand Cañon of the Yellowstone, below Mount Washburne. The famous Jim Bridger doubtless neard of these wonders from trappers or Indians, but it is thought he never visited them. He told of a river that was cold at its source and hot at its mouth. His theory was that the heat was caused by the friction of the water flowing rapidly down such a long, heavy grade. The fact of the hot stream of water has been verified, but the theory, like many others, exploded.

Captain W. W. Delacy and a party of prospectors were in Lower Geyser Basin in 1863. Bart Henderson, Adam Miller, George Houston, C. J. Baronette, Fred. Bottler, S. H. Sprague, and other prospectors visited this region prior to 1869. They gave accounts of what they had seen, but their reports were listened to as idle tales. In 1869 Messrs. Cook and Folsom made a tour of the Yellowstone and Firehole regions.

LITERATURE OF THE PARK.

The first publication relative to the Firehole region that I have seen is that quoted by W. W. Wylie, from the Montana *Post*. It is a communication dated at Yellowstone City, Montana, August 18, 1867, and written by Davis Willson, now of Bozeman, giving an account, at second-hand, of a party of stampeders who went as far up as the Yellowstone Lake. The article is a curiosity. It has been affirmed that Cook and Folsom, who gave a verbal account of their explorations to Surveyor-general Washburne, of Montana, also published an account of their trip in a magazine at Chicago, Illinois, but I have never seen it.

In 1870 the Washburne party visited Wonderland, and N. P. Langford published an account of it in *Scribner's Monthly*. The report of Lieutenant Doane, who accompanied the expedition, was published by the Government. Following these were Professor Hayden's published reports in 1871–2; and soon after this, Richardson's "Wonders of the Upper Yellowstone."

Among other books descriptive of the Park that I have seen are "Wonderland," by Harry Norton (1872); "The Yellowstone National Park," by W. W. Wylie (1882); "The Yellowstone National Park," by Henry J. Windsor (1883); "The Enchanted Land," by R. E. Strahorn (1881); "Calumut of the Coteau," by P. W. Norris (1883). See also annual reports of Superintendents of the Park, published in pamphlet form by the Government, from 1878 to 1883; especially those of P. W. Norris, which contain maps and cuts, and much valuable information.

THE BEST TIME TO VISIT THE PARK

Is in August and the early part of September. The trip can be made in July, and even in June; but the flies and mosquitoes are very troublesome, and the melting snows render the streams, where not bridged, difficult to cross. September is a good time to go, were it not for the equinoctial storm that generally comes about this season. Just after the storm, there is usually a spell of fine weather, which many take advantage of and visit Wonderland, even as late as October, though nights get pretty cool then, and there is danger of a snow-storm. The weather in July and August is almost uniformly good.

TIME REQUIRED TO MAKE THE ROUNDS.

If in great haste—which, however, the tourist should be sure to avoid, as this is *the* trip of a life-time—the Geyser Basins, Yellowstone Falls, Lake, and Cañon, and a few other places, can be visited in a stay of from five to seven days in the Park; *i. e.*, if you go by public conveyance. But do not think of spending less than ten or twelve days, and twenty if possible. If you have your own conveyance, you should spend at least fifteen or twenty days, or even longer, in the Park.

OUTFIT.

This will depend upon how you expect to travel. If by public conveyance, which in time will prove cheapest and most convenient for persons from a distance, you will need little else than plenty of strong and warm woolen clothing, and money sufficient to pay your bills. If you have your own conveyance, be sure to take plenty of good warm clothing and good bedding, with rubber blankets to spread on the ground to keep out dampness. The nights are usually very cool. The brush and fallen timber are hard on clothing, and the hot water and mud, as well as the rocky paths to clamber up and down, will test the endurance of your boots. You can get along very well without liquors, as the atmosphere is so pure and stimulating; but be sure to lay in *a good supply of substantial food*, such as tea, coffee, sugar, canned milk, bacon, flour, yeast-powder, dried fruits, etc. After you have made the most liberal estimates, then you can safely *increase the amount by one-third or one-half*. I have never heard any one complain of having too much food, clothing, or bedding, but many have complained of not having enough. You will need your fishing-tackle, but will have little use for fire-arms. Take smoked glass or a pair of goggles, as the hot sun reflecting from the water, and the hard, stony surface about the springs, is very severe on the eyes.

LIST OF PRICES.

For the benefit of those who may desire to purchase or hire outfits with which to make the tour, the following list of prices is given, which will approximate correctness:

Saddle-ponies,	$30 00 to	$70 00
Pack-animals,	30 00 to	50 00
Saddles,	12 00 to	25 00
Pack-saddles,	3 00 to	5 00
Wagon,	100 00 to	140 00
Harness (set),	20 00 to	40 00
Team horses (each),	75 00 to	100 00
Tents (each),	12 00 to	15 00
Blankets (per pair),	5 00 to	10 00
Hire of saddle-horse (per day),	1 00 to	2 00
Hire of pack-animal (per day),	1 00 to	1 50
Cook, guide, and packer (per day),	3 00 to	5 00
Buggy and driver (per day),	4 00 to	5 00
Flour (per hundred-weight),	2 50 to	4 00
Beans (per pound),	10 to	15
Coffee (per pound),	25 to	35
Tea (per pound),	40 to	1 25
Rice (per pound),	12 to	15
Dried fruit (per pound),	15 to	20
Yeast powder (per pound),	40 to	45
Bacon (per pound),	22 to	25
Board at hotel (per day),	3 00 to	5 00
Bedding, tent and board (per day),	3 00 to	4 00
3-seat carriage and driver (per day),		8 00
2-seat carriage and driver (per day),		7 00

Outfits can be obtained at Virginia City, Bozeman, Mammoth Springs, or of G. W. Marshall, in Firehole Basin, in almost any shape desirable.

You can buy or hire teams, saddle or pack horses, tents, bedding, provisions, for any length of time just as you prefer. Prices for articles purchased may be a shade higher in the Park than outside. People do not all go there for their health alone.

SIZE AND SELECTION OF PARTIES.

Parties of from four to six or eight persons are preferable, and they should be selected with great care, and a mutual understanding had as to the part each one is to perforn on the trip. You will have great need of patience and forbearance, for camp-life tries human nature.

GUIDES

Are not as much needed as formerly; but those expecting to travel much on horseback will need a man to do the packing, and it is well to get one who can perform both offices, and cook too, for that matter.

It will not be difficult to get men who will furnish saddle and pack animals, bedding, and board to persons wishing to visit special points.

THE COST OF TRIP TO PARK

Has been greatly reduced within the last few years. The trip from St. Paul, Omaha, or Kansas City, to and through the Park, including a stay of ten or twelve days, can be made for about $165 or $200, including price of a round-trip ticket ($90), stage fare through the Park ($25), and board at four or five dollars per day ($50). See list of prices on pages 189–190.

THE DISTANCES

As given on pages 213–217 are taken mostly from figures published by P. W. Norris, ex-Superintendent of the Park, and are supposed to approximate correctness, though in several cases I think the tourist will consider the miles pretty long ones.

SUPERINTENDENTS OF THE PARK.

N. P. Langford was the first Superintendent of the Yellowstone National Park. He received his appointment soon after the passage of the act by Congress withdrawing it from the public domain. He was succeeded by P. W. Norris in 1877. Mr. Norris was very active in making new explorations, opening up new trails and bridle-paths, building wagon-roads, and disseminating intelligence relative to the Park. He was succeeded in 1882 by Mr. P. H. Congor, the present incumbent, who will do all in his power for the comfort and welfare of his thousands of guests. The Superintendent and his assistants are supported by a salary from the Government, and an appropriation is made each year by Congress to make such improvements as are deemed necessary, and to keep the roads in repair. The annual appropriation has varied from $10,000 to $15,000.

THE SUPERINTENDENT'S HEAD-QUARTERS

Are at Mammoth Hot Springs, where that officer resides in a log-building on a mound or hill of considerable height near the springs. There are also some Government buildings at Firehole Basin. Congress has recently made provision for the appointment of Assistant Superintendents, who are to aid in securing observance of

THE RULES AND REGULATIONS OF THE PARK.

A letter from the Superintendent of the Park at Mammoth Hot Springs, dated April 22, 1884, states the following synopsis of the present rules:

"All hunting is prohibited, and the wounding or killing of game or any bird; and no fish is to be taken in the Park, except with hook and line. No specimens are to be collected, nor the formations or incrustations about the springs, geysers, or any other natural curiosities, in any manner to be defaced nor disturbed. Particular caution to be had in regard to camp-fires. All fires are to be extinguished before leaving camp. I suppose that these rules will be revised and amended immediately after the present session of Congress.

"P. H. CONGOR, *Superintendent.*"

Though these rules are subject to change, as will be seen,

yet the above will give the reader an idea of their nature and intent.

HOW TO REACH THE PARK.

The tourist in the East or South, desiring to visit Wonderland, can take choice of the two great Pacific railway lines, known as the Southern and Northern routes. The first is from Kansas City, over the Kansas Pacific *via* Denver and Cheyenne; or from Omaha *via* Union Pacific to Ogden, Utah; thence by the Utah Northern to Beaver Cañon, Idaho, where he takes the stage, or private conveyance, up the Snake River Valley to the Lower Firehole Basin, one hundred miles from the railroad. Or, he can follow the railroad northward from Beaver Cañon to Dillon, then take stage to Virginia City, Montana (sixty-five miles), and thence by private conveyance up the Madison Valley to Lower Firehole Basin, in the Park, ninety-five miles farther. Or, if desirable to see more of Montana Territory, he can follow the Utah Northern on *via* Silver Bow Junction (stopping over at Butte) to Garrison, where he takes the Northern Pacific eastward *via* Helena and Bozeman to Livingstone, and thence to the Park.

The Northern route is by the Northern Pacific from St. Paul to Livingstone, thence up the Yellowstone Valley *via* the National Park Branch Railway to its terminus at the border of the Park, where a stage line connects with trains, taking passengers over the mountain to Mammoth Hot Springs, eight miles distant.

Each of these routes has its advantages, and each offers reduced rates to tourists, which are given below.

By taking the Southern route the tourist can see the "Great Plains," visit Denver and other interesting points in Colorado, also Cheyenne, and the Great Salt Lake. It involves a stage ride of two days from Beaver Cañon to Firehole Basin. But the officers of this route will do all in their power for the accommodation and comfort of tourists.

The Northern route offers an "All Rail Line," and somewhat shorter route, to the boundary line of the Park. Those who desire can come by one route and return by the other—enter the Park at Mammoth Springs and leave at Firehole Basin via stage and Utah Northern Railway, or *vice versa*.

To those who live in the South or South-west the Southern route is preferable.

Tourists from San Francisco can reach the Park *via* the Central Pacific to Ogden, thence over the Utah Northern Railway, and from Portland, Oregon, by way of the Northern Pacific eastward to Livingstone, and thence as above described to the Park.

The following will give

ROUND-TRIP RATES TO FIREHOLE BASIN VIA UNION PACIFIC RAILWAY.

"OMAHA, NEBRASKA, April 5, 1884.

"E. J. STANLEY, ESQ.—*Dear Sir:* Please find herewith list of round-trip rates from Omaha or Kansas City to Firehole Basin and return, the point to which we ticket our Yellowstone passengers:

Party of 1 to 5 . . . . . $90 00 each.
Party of 5 to 15 . . . . . . 85 00 each.
Party of 15 to 25 . . . . . 80 00 each.
Party of 25 to 50 . . . . . . 75 00 each.
Party of 50 to 75 . . . . . 70 00 each.
Party of 75 to 100 . . . . . . 65 00 each.
Party of 100 or more . . . . . 60 00 each.
Rate from Ogden . . . . 45 00 each.

"Tickets will be placed on sale June 1—good to return until September 30, with usual stop-over privileges. Above rates are made *via* Beaver Cañon only. Yours truly,

"C. S. STEBBINS, *G. T. A.*"

Parties holding first-class tickets to and beyond Ogden, going East or West, can purchase round-trip tickets from Ogden to Firehole Basin, Yellowstone Park, and return *via* Beaver Cañon, for $45. Fare (round trip) from Beaver Cañon to Firehole Basin, over Bassett Brothers stage line, $25. Round-trip tickets from Omaha, Leavenworth, St. Joseph, or Kansas City, to San Francisco, $100 to $180—according to size of party. For additional information, inquire of C. S. Stebbins, General Ticket Agent Union Pacific Railway, Omaha, Nebraska.

NORTHERN PACIFIC RATES TO MAMMOTH HOT SPRINGS.

Regular rate (one way), St. Paul, Minneapolis, or Duluth, to Mammoth Hot Springs, $59.20.

Regular rate (one way), Portland, Oregon, to Mammoth Hot Springs, $66.45.

Round-trip tourist rates from St. Paul, Minneapolis, Duluth, or Portland, to Yellowstone National Park Hotel, at Mammoth Hot Springs, and return—*just the same as those given in above table.*

Tickets on sale June 1; good until September 30—with usual stop-over privileges.

For full particulars, address J. R. Berry, General Tourist Agent, Chicago, Illinois; any authorized agent of the Northern Pacific Railway, or Charles S. Fee, General Passenger Agent, St. Paul, Minn.

A DAILY LINE OF STAGES IS IN OPERATION

From Mammoth Hot Springs, making the grand rounds to all the principal objects of interest in the Park. The fare for the round trip through the Park is $25. The trip can be made in from five to seven days—just owing to the time spent in sight-seeing.

ACCOMMODATIONS IN THE PARK

Are much better than formerly. By permission from Congress, the Secretary of the Interior has executed a lease to the Yellowstone National Park Improvement Company (or Rufus Hatch & Co.), at a nominal rent, ten acres of ground at different points in the Park for hotel purposes for ten years, distributed as follows: Two acres near Mammoth Hot Springs; one and one-half acre at Upper Geyser Basin, east of Old Faithful Geyser; one and one-half acre on Madison River, near western boundary of Park; one acre just east of Soda

Springs; one and one-half acre just east of Tower Falls; one and one-half acre near the head of the Grand Cañon and Falls of Yellowstone; and one acre on the bank of Yellowstone Lake, near the outlet. The Secretary of the Interior is to be advised with in regard to the character of buildings and outhouses erected thereon; and the prices for accommodations are to be submitted for his approval; and he is also to have the privilege of leasing ground for similar purposes to other parties, thus preventing a monopoly. The company is required to build a fine hotel at Mammoth Hot Springs, which is to cost not less (with appurtenances) than one hundred and fifty thousand dollars. An elegant and commodious building was erected at this place last spring, which is said to be quite similar to the famous Hotel La Fayette, of Lake Minnetonka. It has two hundred and fifty rooms, is to be furnished with electric lights, and its accommodations are expected to be first-class in every particular. It will be open in good season for the summer's travel.

Mr. G. W. Marshall has a good hotel at the forks of Firehole River, in the Lower Geyser (or Firehole) Basin, which will accommodate thirty or forty guests.

Last year the Park Company had boarding and lodging tents, made of heavy canvas, in Upper Geyser Basin and at the Great Falls of the Yellowstone. They will doubtless erect hotels at all the points designated in the lease, and the tourist will thus be comfortably provided for at any point of interest in the Park during the coming season.

ROUTES TO THE PARK BY WAGON OR HORSEBACK.

While parties from a distance will visit Wonderland by rail and stage, yet many who live near by will prefer to go by their own conveyance, which is less expensive and far more satisfactory, as there need be no hurry to rush through. One route of this character, available for persons going from Snake River Valley, is by the stage line from Beaver Cañon. The route is natural and easy: up a branch of Snake River, through a good pass, to Lower Geyser Basin—ninety-eight or one hundred miles. The next is that from Virginia City to Lower Geyser Basin. This leaves Virginia City at the south-east side, leads over a divide to Madison River (a beautiful stream seventy-five yards in width), and follows up the valley, crossing and recrossing the river. About forty-two miles from Virginia City it leaves the river to the left, leads through a pass to the right, crossing the main range of the Rocky Mountains, where a splendid view of the surrounding country is obtained. The Three Tetons loom up grandly to the south-west. A short ride brings you to Henry's Lake, a beautiful sheet of water two miles wide by five in length, with low pebbly and grassy shores, and surrounded by romantic peaks, and is almost within five hundred feet of the summit of the Rockies, on the Pacific slope. Its surface is flecked with water-fowl, and its waters are full of excellent salmon-trout, with which a Mr. Sawtelle has for years furnished the market at Virginia City, and other points in Montana. It is sixty miles from Virginia City—a day and a half's ride—and a splendid place to camp and fish, and enjoy the inspiration of the surrounding scenery. The mountains are full of large game. The road from here turns eastward, crosses the main range again to the Upper Madison Valley, and about fifteen miles from Henry's Lake the south fork of the Madison River is crossed, where there is a good camp. About two miles from here the traveler enters the Park from the west, and a ride of ten miles or more over a splendid road, with the Madison River on the left, brings you to Riverside, twenty-two miles from Henry's Lake, and a fine camp. From here there is one (the old) road leading up the river through the cañon; the other leads over a very steep mountain to the right. The mountain-road now takes precedence, as it saves fording the river several times. The summit furnishes another fine view of the surrounding scenery. It is about twelve miles from Riverside to Marshall's Hotel, in Firehole Basin, over the mountain, and a little less by the river route.

The other route is from Bozeman to Mammoth Hot Springs. This is easily found, as it leads by a good road south-easterly from Bozeman, through a deep mountain gorge, over a divide, then down Trail Creek to the Yellowstone Valley, and up the river and valley past Bottler's Ranch to Mammoth Springs, seventy-five miles from Bozeman. Most of this route has been described in "Rambles."

Parties going by private conveyance would do well to take along with their wagons a few saddles, one or two extra saddle-animals, and a pack-saddle or two. They are a great convenience in visiting places off the main routes, where wagons cannot be taken. Where several gentlemen go together, they often prefer to make the entire trip on horseback, carrying their baggage on pack-animals. This is a very independent mode of traveling.

Choice of routes to the Park will depend largely upon the point where you start from. If you enter by Virginia City and Henry's Lake, it is well to return by Bozeman; and if you enter by Bozeman and Mammoth Springs, it is well, if not too inconvenient, to return the other way. The advantage of going by Mammoth Springs, if any difference, is that the tourist sees the wonders of the Park more in their natural order. The first sight of Mammoth Springs removes all his misgivings, he feels amply repaid for coming, and his appetite is whetted for other wonders. Leaving the springs, after exploring its adjacent curiosities, he is led by Obsidian Cliffs, Norris Geyser Basin, Monument Geyser and Point Pots, Gibbon Cañon and Falls, Lower and Middle Geyser Basins, right up to the grand geysers of the world in Upper Firehole Basin. All this time curiosity has been on tiptoe, and he has enjoyed seeing many things which will appear tame after a visit to the geysers. He now seeks refreshment along the shores of Yellowstone Lake and River, at the Great Falls and Grand Cañon (the finest scene in the entire Park), on top of Mount Washburne, fishing at Tower Falls; returning by Fossil Forest and East Gardner Falls to the springs.

Or, if preferable, he can enter at Lower Geyser Basin, go to Upper Geyser Basin, Yellowstone Lake, Great Falls and Grand Cañon of the Yellowstone, Mount Washburne, Tower Falls, Fossil Forest, East Gardiner Falls, and Mammoth Spring, then return by Obsidian Cliffs, Norris Geyser Basin, Gibbon Falls and Cañon, to Lower Geyser Basin. Or, he can just reverse this order if he chooses, and go first to Norris Basin, Mammoth Springs, Tower Falls, Great Falls and Cañon, Lake, and back to Upper Geyser Basin.

ROUTES WITHIN THE PARK.

From Mammoth Springs to the Geyser Basins.

As the trip described in "Rambles in Wonderland" commenced at Mammoth Springs, it was thought the more natural way to commence these notes at the same place. If the tourist should enter the Park at the Lower Geyser Basin, or other points, the notes and distances as given can be easily made to answer the same purpose. The first point to be noticed is

THE MAMMOTH HOT SPRINGS, for a description of which see "Rambles," pages 54–61. There have been many changes here since 1873, notable among which are the head-quarters building on the hill and the splendid hotel and out-buildings. On the bank of that clear stream, coming in from the right, up in the edge of the pines, is where we had our tents pitched. The Liberty Cap still stands, and also the Bee-hive just above it, which has changed its name to Giant's or Devil's Thumb. There are good conveniences for bathing. Two or three days, or more, can be profitably spent here visiting adjacent peaks, cañons, and water-falls. A half or a whole day can be profitably spent visiting

THE MIDDLE GARDINER FALLS AND CAÑON, which are reached by a bridle-path leading nearly due south, about four miles from the springs. The cataract falls about three hundred feet, one-third of which is perpendicular. The cañon is from twelve hundred to fifteen hundred feet deep, and in its gorgeous coloring and wonderful carving resembles somewhat the Grand Cañon of the Yellowstone. The falls and cañon are well worth seeing. Two miles above the falls, in the cañon to the south-west, are the

SHEEP EATER CLIFFS, along the base of which are what is supposed to have been the haunts of the Sheep Eater Indians, who inhabited these mountain fastnesses years ago. And about three miles from the falls, following an intricate trail over the rocks and through the timber to the south-west, you will reach the wagon-road leading to the Geyser Basins.

DEPARTURE FROM THE SPRINGS. The road starts near the Devil's Thumb and leads up the steep face of Terrace Mountain for two miles to the summit. The grade is good, but very steep in places, and requires nearly half a day, with frequent resting of team, if loaded, to reach the top. The altitude is three thousand feet above the hotel. Much of the way is through a dense growth of timber. From the summit a slight descent is made, and a turn to the left through an open valley and a ride of three miles brings you to Swan Lake, a good camping place on the right, five miles from the springs. By turning to the left two and one-quarter miles from the summit, and following a trail half a mile, at the head of the cañon on West Gardiner River, you will find a beautiful cascade called Rustic Falls. The river tumbles nearly sixty feet over a precipice. The banks are lined with ferns, and the scene is picturesque and captivating.

About two and one-fourth miles from Swan Lake, the Middle Gardiner is crossed, and one mile farther on is Indian Creek. About five miles from here to the west is Bell's Peak. The general course of the road from the summit of Terrace Mountain is southward. Follow up Obsidian Creek to upper end of

WILLOW PARK, which is eleven miles from the springs. Plenty of wood, grass, and good water, but no fish in the streams. Camp here. Some good cold springs on the right one mile above here, the last good water for five or ten miles, except Lake of the Woods, which is only passable.

OBSIDIAN CLIFFS AND BEAVER LAKE are two miles farther on. The cliffs are composed of volcanic glass, mostly black, except some of a reddish hue at the southern end. They rise in columns from one hundred to two hundred and fifty feet along the mountain. The grade along their base was made by building fires upon the great blocks of glass, heating and then throwing cold water upon them to fracture them; after which they were pounded down with sledge-hammers. These cliffs are quite a curiosity. The Indians manufactured their arrow-heads from this material, small bits of which are found all through the Park. *Beaver Lake* lies on the right of the road, and is fed by the poisonous waters of Green Creek, which enter from the right toward the upper, or southern, end. The road from here leads up a steep grade, passing some nauseous brimstone springs on the right, to the summit of the divide between the Yellowstone and Madison rivers, where a fine view is obtained of the lofty mountains to the west and north-west. Just over the summit to the left of the road is

LAKE OF THE WOODS, so named because it is surrounded by towering pines, whose lofty shadows are reflected in its crystal depths.

NORRIS VALLEY, a nice grassy park, is two miles farther on. Three miles from here is the crossing of the Norris Fork of the Gibbon River, where it is advisable to make camp from which to explore the wonders of

NORRIS GEYSER BASIN, which is one-half mile farther south, on each side of the road. Here are the first geysers to be seen on this route, and the beholder is apt to be astonished above measure. Clouds of steam and jets and columns of water are ascending constantly. Springs and great gurgling, surging caldrons are boiling and fussing and sputtering, and subterranean thunderings and rumblings, like the noise of heavy machinery, are coming up constantly. This is one of the oldest geyser basins in the Park, but it seems to be declining in activity and power. The numerous springs furnish many shades of color—yellow, blue, and black. On the right of the road to the south-west is the "Constant," then the "Twins" and "Triplets," which are spouting almost constantly; and farther along on the same side, on the ridge, is a caldron which throws out a great quantity of a muddy, paint-like substance, having a leaden hue, several feet high. It acts about every fifteen or twenty minutes. Another crater near this one sends out vast quantities of super-heated steam, and is called "Steam-boat Vent."

On the left of the road, a few rods from the mud caldron, is the "Emerald Pool," a large emerald-tinted basin, with coral-like sides, filled with water clear as crystal, making it an object of indescribable beauty. Then there is the "Minute-man," at the foot of the ridge, spouting a six-inch jet every sixty seconds to the height of say twenty-five feet. Still farther to the east and south is the "Monarch" of the basin, which daily sends up a splendid column of hot water to the height of about one hundred feet. On the left, soon after entering the basin, is one which Colonel P. W. Norris describes as "a geyser of erratic habits and irregular periods of eruption of its column of waters, which is sometimes one hundred feet high, but usually much less." There is also the "Vixen," the "Fearless," and others of less importance, in this basin. About four miles from the last camp we come to

ELK PARK, OR GIBBON BASIN, OR MEADOWS, as it has been variously called, which is a park about five miles in extent, surrounded by mountains which are covered with timber. It is a fine place to camp, and tourists should not attempt to go farther if it is late in the day, as there is no grass on the route between here and the Lower Geyser Basin, fifteen miles distant. Two objects of interest are near here.

THE PAINT POTS are found in an opening in the timber, about half a mile eastward around a bluff, and consist of several boiling springs which cast out a paste-like substance of every hue and tint imaginable. One of the springs is red as blood, and has been called "Blood Geyser." The great column of steam constantly rising will indicate the locality of this group, and the singular phenomena will amply repay you for the trouble of a visit. You should be sure to visit

MONUMENT GEYSER BASIN. Just at the head of Gibbon Cañon, after leaving camp, there is a foot-bridge over Gibbon River, on the right of the road, to a trail on the opposite bank of the stream, following which, over the steep ascent of Mount Schurz, this basin is reached, one mile distant, at an elevation of one thousand feet above the river-bed. The trip can be made on horseback, if you are careful to avoid getting your horse's feet scalded at the bank in crossing the river. There are several acres in the basin, and a dozen or more of the springs are surrounded by grotesque formations like monuments, varying from four or five to fifteen feet in height. Some resemble chimneys, some wild animals, and others send out volumes of steam, smoke, and heated air, with whizzing, rushing sounds that fill you with terror, and may be heard for miles. There are also caldrons of boiling sulphur, and many other objects of interest. The view of the surrounding landscape is quite enjoyable, and amply compensates for the trip.

GIBBON CAÑON. The wagon-road follows through this wonderful gorge for several miles, amid small geysers and boiling springs, which spurt and bubble up along both sides of the river. The overhanging walls, towering up at one place to a height of two thousand feet, present a scene of rugged grandeur seldom witnessed. The road leads by a gradual grade from the river to the top of the cañon on the left opposite

THE GIBBON FALLS, which are four miles from the head of the cañon. They are reached by a trail on the right of the road leading down the steep declivity to the very brink. There is another trail that leads to the foot of the falls. The water tumbles eighty feet over a cliff, and presents a lively and enchanting view. Passing Cañon Creek, two and one-half miles below the falls, and Earthquake Cliffs, five miles from the falls, a ride of ten miles (from the falls) over numerous woodland terraces brings you out into

THE LOWER GEYSER BASIN, where you follow up the left bank of Firehole River, take the right-hand road, cross the East Fork, then the West Fork of Firehole River, or cross the main stream just below the forks, and you are at Marshall's Hotel, near the forks of the above-named stream. Here are hotel accommodations for thirty or forty guests, and a supply store. There was a post-office here, but I understand it has been discontinued. The roads from Virginia City, and also from Beaver Cañon, come in at this point. The roads to Upper Geyser Basin and to and from the Yellowstone Lake and Falls converge here. It is quite a road-center, and the tourist can go from here in almost any direction he may choose. You are now so near the great geysers of the world that

THE TEMPTATION becomes very great to hurry right on. But by so doing you will miss many objects of great interest. By seeing them now, your appetite will only be whetted for the greater wonders still ahead, whereas if you wait until the return trip they will not have half the attraction for you. Be sure to stop a day or more here. A good camping place can be found near the hotel, or a mile south, on the same side of the river, in Geyser Meadows. A ride of two miles southward from the hotel, through beautiful grassy openings, skirted by lovely woodlands, will bring you to

QUEEN'S LAUNDRY, a lovely spring, possessing wonderful cleansing properties. There is a large central spring and numerous smaller ones descending in terraces, the water growing cooler as it gets farther from the central spring, which is very hot. It is a good place for a bath. Near here are the

TWIN DOMES, OR BUTTES, the summits of which offer a good view of the Basin. And just beyond these, up the little stream called Fairy Falls Creek, at the foot of the mountain, are the beautiful, the fascinating

FAIRY FALLS, two hundred feet high, a view of which no tourist should miss.

Returning to the hotel, recross the East and West Forks of the Firehole River, follow up the East Fork on the west side one mile, and recross to the south side. This is called Prospect Point. Here there is a blacksmith-shop and other Government buildings. One mile on the road leading southward from Prospect Point is

CAMP REUNION, an old and favorite camping place for the early tourists. It is in the edge of the timber, and by the side of a beautiful little stream of water. We camped here in 1873. On an eminence a short distance to the south of this camp is a group of hot springs, at the southern extremity of which is *Thud Geyser*. This is a very interesting group. South of this a quarter of a mile is another group, among which, on a table-like mound, is the beautiful *Fountain Geyser*. It has a curiously shaped crater, lined with formations resembling cushions, and spouts every day, and sometimes three or four times a day, to a height of forty or sixty feet. A little farther southward from the Fountain is a beaded funnel-like crater, which frequently sends a jet of water ten or fifteen feet high. It is called the *Jet Geyser*. Eastward from the Fountain, beyond some skirting pines and large bowlders, on an eminence, is a great mud caldron, inclosed by a rim several feet high, and known as

THE PAINT POT, OR CHALK VAT, and other appropriate names. It contains a fine paste-like substance of a beautiful white, at the south end, and a delicate pink color at the north end. It is in constant agitation, boiling up in great globules or rings a foot or more high, which burst and send the delicate substance several feet up in the air.

From Camp Reunion follow the road leading southwesterly across the basin, then up the east side of Firehole River three miles, to

MIDWAY GEYSER BASIN, OR HELL'S HALF ACRE. It is on the opposite side of the river, and is reached by a road leading over to it. Do not try to ford while the great geyser just above is in action, if you do not wish to get your horses' feet badly scalded. The most noted spring in this group, which is described in "Rambles" (see pages 94, 95), has become one of the most powerful geysers in the Park. Colonel Norris states that its eruptions in 1880 were most powerful, sending up an immense column of water from one hundred to three hundred feet high, belching out great quantities of rocks, and they were repeated once in each twenty-four hours. It is said to spout oftener now. It was called the "Excelsior" by Colonel Norris, but has since been named by others the "Sheridan," in honor of that distinguished General, who recently visited the Park. The coloring along the streams flowing from this group into the river is most exquisite. After "doing" this basin, return to the main road, follow it up the east side of the Firehole River, over a passable route, five miles, to the

UPPER FIREHOLE BASIN. Pass the Fan Geyser on the right, near the river, and between that and the Riverside just above cross the Firehole River, and follow up the west side. Just a short distance from the crossing, on your right, is the *Grotto Geyser*. Two hundred yards south-west of this is the *Giant*, on the left of the road, which will be readily recognized by the description given in "Rambles" (page 113). About two hundred yards almost west of the Giant, on a white mound of geyserite formation, is the *Splendid*, which is very powerful, and has developed within the last few years. Near the river-bank, a short distance south of the Giant, is a pool about thirty by fifty feet, ornamented with white globular masses, which is called the *Oblong Geyser*, though, from the singular jets of steam shooting out from the main body of water when in action, it has been called the *Comet*. About one-third of a mile above the Giant, near the road, in the edge of timber, on a prominent cone, is the *Castle*, four hundred feet from the river; just north of which, on the same mound, is the beautiful blue spring, sometimes called the

"Devil's Well." Just back of this, to the west, is a good place for a small party to camp, as it is quite central. The little grove on the river-bank, a few hundred yards to the left of the Castle, has also been a favorite camping place. The *Grand Geyser* is located at the base of a bluff, nearly opposite the Castle, five hundred feet east of the river. On the same geyser mound, or platform, is the *Turban*. Southward from the Grand, and not far from the river, is the *Saw-mill*, one of my favorites; and not far away are also the *Bulger*, the *Tardy*, and the *Spasmodic*, which are geysers of lesser note. The *Lion*, *Lioness*, and *Two Cubs* constitute a group of geysers situated on a mound next above the Saw-mill, up and east of the river, a short distance west of the Giantess. The Lioness and the Two Cubs are close together, while the Lion crouches about fifty feet away, and sometimes in his rage sends the boiling water fifty or sixty feet in the air. The wonderful *Giantess* is a short distance eastward, on a sloping mound. A little over one hundred yards distant from the Giantess, south-west, near the foot-bridge, is the beautiful *Bee-hive;* and across the river, on an eminence, southward, standing like a faithful sentinel, is *Old Faithful*, which is a universal favorite.

As the most of the geysers here mentioned, and the principal features of the Upper Geyser Basin, have been described in "Rambles" (see pages 97–116), and as the accompanying table gives names, intervals, and heights of eruptions, as gathered from the most reliable sources available, it is unnecessary here to do more than merely indicate the location, which I have tried briefly to do. The tourist will prefer seeing them with his own eyes to any description that might be attempted with pen or pencil.

Two or three days, at least, should be spent in this basin. Even then you may not see all the geysers in eruption, as they often go off in the night.

A favorite camping place is right west of Old Faithful Geyser, where there is a small park and some grass. But by going three-fourths of a mile south or south-west of Old

Faithful, through the open timber, you will find a large open park with excellent grass and a fine place to picket horses.

TABLE SHOWING INTERVALS OF ERUPTIONS AND HEIGHTS OF DIFFERENT GEYSERS

UPPER GEYSER BASIN.

Name.	Period of Eruption.	Time in Action.	Height of Column.
Old Faithful	55 to 65 minutes.	About 4 minutes.	125 to 150 feet.
Bee-hive	About every 24 hours.	7 to 10 minutes.	About 200 feet.
Giantess	About once a week.	12 hours.	75 to 250 feet.
Lion	Not known.	About 5 minutes.	75 feet.
Lioness	Not known.	About 3 minutes.	60 feet.
Castle	About every 48 hours.	About 30 minutes.	50 to 80 feet.
Grand	Daily or oftener.	15 to 20 minutes.	100 to 200 feet.
Saw-mill	Quite often.	2 to 2½ hours.	15 to 35 feet.
Splendid	Each 3 or 4 hours.	4 to 10 minutes.	150 to 200 feet.
Grotto	Each 4 or 5 hours.	5 to 15 minutes.	25 to 50 feet.
Giant	Once in 3 or 4 days.	About 1½ hour.	100 to 200 feet.
Fan	3 times a day.	8 to 15 minutes.	About 60 feet.
Riverside	3 times a day.	10 to 15 minutes.	About 60 feet.

MIDWAY GEYSER BASIN.

Excelsior, or Sheridan	Each 3 or 4 hours.	3 to 5 minutes.	50 to 250 feet.

LOWER GEYSER BASIN.

Fountain	Each day or oftener.	5 to 15 minutes.	50 to 100 feet.

NORRIS GEYSER BASIN.

Monarch	Daily.	20 to 30 minutes.	50 to 100 feet.
Minute-man	Each minute.	A half minute.	20 to 30 feet.

FROM UPPER GEYSER BASIN TO YELLOWSTONE LAKE there are two routes. If you are in a vehicle you will have to return to the Lower Basin, but if on horseback it is well to go by the

UPPER FIREHOLE AND SHOSHONE LAKE TRAIL, over which there will perhaps be a wagon-road at some future time. If you choose this route, take the trail past Old Faithful, follow up the river, and nearly one mile up cross to the east side. Nearly two miles distant are

KEPLER'S OR FIREHOLE FALLS, a lovely retreat, where the principal cataract is perhaps forty feet high. Six miles farther on eastward the trail crosses the main range of the Rockies, through Norris Pass, after which it follows down a steep mountain to

DELACY'S CREEK AND CAMP, two miles south of which is

SHOSHONE LAKE, six miles in length and four and a half in width on an average, but at some places is very narrow. Its outlet is a tributary of Snake River, and its surface lower than the Yellowstone Lake. It affords many good camping places, but its waters contain no fish. At the south-western extremity of the lake are a number of geyser springs.

Following the trail eastward from the crossing of Delacy Creek, a ride of three miles through the timber up the mountain brings you again to the summit of the main divide, near

Two Ocean Pond, on the left; and another three-mile jaunt down the steep mountain, on the Atlantic slope, and you are at

Hot Spring Camp, on the extreme western arm or thumb of Yellowstone Lake. This is a very interesting and most remarkable region. Oddly formed craters, some of which protrude into the lake, springs of every size, shape, depth, color, temperature, and consistency simmer and sizzle and spout and gurgle and boil and bubble away without intermission. One of the springs is three hundred feet deep. You can look down into the fairy depths of some of them to a great distance. There are "paint pools" and "paint pots" here that possibly surpass any hitherto visited. Streams of hot water can be seen bubbling up away out in the lake, quite a distance from the shore. The noted "Steam-boat Springs," on the northern end of the lake, east of the outlet, can be seen from here. The funnel-shaped craters of some of these springs stand so far out into the lake as to form a real peninsula; and you can actually stand on these cones and catch trout and cook them without moving from your tracks or taking the fish from the hook. This is no fish story; it has been tested frequently.

Heart Lake and Mount Sheridan, which afford some fine views, can be reached by a ride of from ten to twenty miles from this camp; but there is no trail, and the fallen timber is so dense that it is not advisable to try it.

Leaving the camp at Hot Springs, the trail leads northward, traverses a firehole basin, leads over a high bluff to a hot spring creek, six and a half miles distant, where there is a poor camp, and the timber is too thick to picket a horse with safety. From here it is six miles north to the famous

Natural Bridge, which is on a small creek, about one

and one-half mile from the trail, to the left. It is a natural causeway over a small stream (Bridge Creek), and is about five feet wide, twenty-nine feet long, and eighty feet from top to bottom on the lower side. It has natural balustrades on the side, has been used by the large game for crossing, and there is a trail leading over so that the tourist can ride across if he desires to do so. Colonel Norris says that it was once the brink of a cataract which has been undermined by the water, thus leaving a natural arch. It is well worth a visit.

From the bridge the tourist has a delightful ride near the shore of the lake to the outlet, five miles distant, where there is a good camp, and where is the present terminus of the wagon-road, which is described in the

WAGON-ROAD FROM LOWER GEYSER BASIN TO YELLOWSTONE LAKE AND GREAT FALLS AND GRAND CANON OF THE YELLOWSTONE.

Return from the upper to the lower basin over the route followed going up. The road passes through a gap near Prospect Point and Camp Reunion. This is where Cowan and party were captured by the Nez Perces in 1877. (See "Rambles," page 158). From here the road leads eastward up the general course of the East Fork of the Firehole River, which it crosses several times. At Rock Fork, five miles, is a good camp, and also at Willow Camp, seven miles. Plenty of wood, good water, and grass for stock. No fish. It is nearly ten miles to the foot of the steep mountain near where Cowan and party were fired upon by the Indians.

After climbing the long, steep, and densely wooded mountain to the divide, a fine view is obtained of the surrounding landscape.

MARY'S LAKE, a beautiful sheet of water about one-fourth of a mile across, is passed to the right of the road a little farther on. Its water, though beautiful to look at, is brackish. Chief Joseph camped just east of here in 1877, the night after taking Mrs. Cowan, her sister and brother prisoners. His fortifications can be seen yet.

The route from here eastward leads amid numerous sulphur and other hot springs. Three miles from Mary's Lake, on a small stream coming down from the right, is a grassy cove and a good camp. Water passable. Fish found in some of the adjacent streams. An interesting group of hot springs just down the stream to the left, which are mentioned in "Rambles." (See page 89.)

From here the road follows almost due east over a rolling, open country, known as Hayden Valley (see "Rambles," page 82), seven miles eastward to the old trail leading up the Yellowstone River. Keep the right-hand road, and two miles farther will bring you to a good camp just to the left of

MUD SPRINGS AND MUD VOLCANO. The Muddy Geyser, described in "Rambles," is now inactive, but the volcano will be recognized by the mud on the trees around it, and so will another spring just below called the Belcher or Belching Spring. Near here is the Nez Perce Ford, the best on the river, and where the Nez Perce Indians, under Joseph, crossed in 1877, when they were every moment expecting an attack from the troops under General Howard. And just east of the river is where Mrs. Cowan, her sister, and her brother Frank Carpenter, were released, crossed back to this side—the water almost swimming their horses—and were told by the chief to "go quick;" which command they were not reluctant to obey. (See "Rambles," pages 164–165.) It was at this camp that our horses played truant, and it took Judge Knowles and myself half a day to find them where they had rambled away off the wooded mountains to the south-west.

From here it is six miles up the Yellowstone River to the foot of the lake. The road follows near the river, and the scenery is enchanting. Parties often divide at Upper Basin, some bringing wagons by this route, others going on horseback by Shoshone Pass. Here is the meeting-place. Fine camp. A week can be spent very pleasantly. Hotel accommodations are to be furnished here by the Yellowstone Park Improvement Company, which will be at no distant day. And there will doubtless be sail-boats for those desiring a voyage over the lake.

FROM YELLOWSTONE LAKE TO THE FALLS.

Return from lake to the forks of the road, two miles north of Mud Geyser. One and a half mile north of here, over an open sage-brush country, is

SULPHUR MOUNTAIN, which has been described in "Rambles," page 83. There has been but little change, except that the Sulphur Spring at the base of the mountain has lost much of its beauty. Major Freeman, of the United States Army, declared that spring to be "the prettiest thing in the entire Park." Be sure to see the very interesting mud springs which are some distance through the timber, southeast from the big sulphur spring.

From Sulphur Mountain to the Falls, northward, is six miles or more, crossing Alum Creek on the way. The water of Alum Creek is strongly impregnated with alum. The wagon-road extends to a point near the Upper Falls. About a mile or two south of here, on a little creek, may be found the remains of the camp of the Helena party, which was attacked by Indians in 1877. At the camp at the terminus of the road Colonel Norris found an inscription on a tree twenty inches in diameter, about four feet from the ground—"J. O. R., Aug. 29, 1819"—which is still legible.

THE GREAT FALLS AND GRAND CAÑON have been so fully described in "Rambles," pages 71-80, that it is necessary to say but little here. They continue to be among the greatest attractions of Wonderland, and are engaging the attention of some of the finest artists of the world. A fine painting of the cañon and falls, by Moran, adorns the walls of the Capitol building at Washington.

PROSPECT POINT, one mile below the lower falls, affords one of the finest views of the cañon. Descent to the water's edge can be made from a point just above this place; but it is very dangerous, and I would advise you not to try it. By following a trail just west of a little stream near this point, through the timber a few hundred yards from the cañon, you will find an excellent camping ground, which is quite handy to all the points of interest. At the brink of the Lower Falls a railing of poles has been prepared, from which you can peer into the seething depths below.

THE CRYSTAL FALLS of Cascade Creek are about midway between the Upper and Lower Falls, and are formed by the water tumbling over a succession of ledges, one fifty, and another about twenty feet in height, above and below the narrow bridge that spans the stream. Grotto Pool is just below the bridge. Following the creek down to the mouth you will find excellent fishing in the river between the Upper and Lower Falls.

It is well for the tourist, if he has time, to follow the brink of the Grand Cañon down for several miles, as there is much in the fantastic shapes and exquisite coloring of the great towering walls that is worth while to see. Three or four miles down, on the opposite side of the river, a creek drops into the cañon at a great depth, and makes a beautiful water-fall.

SAFETY-VALVE GEYSER AND PAINTED CLIFFS. Three or four miles below this, from the lower end of a meadow to the right, the bridle-path leads through a pine forest by a steep descent to a small geyser with the name given above. Another steep descent leads to the river underneath the Painted Cliffs, which are perhaps fifteen hundred feet in height, and rather interesting and peculiar. "This," says Colonel Norris, "is the only place between the mouth of Tower Creek and Lower Falls where the descent can be made to the river." Although the fishing is fine, yet it is not advisable to try it. None but the most venturesome will dare go, and then they are not apt to be paid for the time and trouble of the climb.

FROM THE GREAT FALLS TO TOWER CREEK FALLS there are two routes: one a bridle-path, which skirts along down the brink of the Grand Cañon for about four miles, then turns to the left across the eastern base of Mount Washburne, and follows down the long grassy ridge to Tower Falls; the other, the old trail which leaves the Upper Falls, turning to the left from near Cascade Creek, follows for a distance along the general course of that stream, then through fallen timber skirting Dunraven's Peak to the left, and up over the western base of Mount Washburne, and thence northward to the falls. The latter is considered the best route. It is seventeen miles by the former and fifteen miles by the latter route.

MOUNT WASHBURNE can be reached on horseback from the highest point on either trail, and no tourist should fail to go to the top, which is only about one mile from the trail. The view is extremely grand and inspiring. (See "Rambles," pages 68-71.) A wagon-road will doubtless be constructed from the Great Falls to Tower Falls erelong, which will be a great convenience. At

TOWER FALLS there is a splendid camping place, with plenty of wood, the purest water, and fine grass convenient—about two hundred yards above the falls south of the creek. A good view can be obtained from a towering cliff overhanging the falls; but it is best to go to the mouth of the creek at Yellowstone River and follow up through the deep gorge over the rocks and fallen trees, which will enable you to get right at the foot of the charmingly beautiful cascade. You will be loath to leave this delightful retreat. The writer gathered a fine mess of raspberries in the cañon on the south side of the creek during his visit there. The ascent or descent can be made by a trail a short distance below the falls, but it is very steep. Splendid fishing at the mouth of the creek. (See "Rambles," pages 64, 65.)

There is a bridge over this stream near the camp, crossing which the trail leads up a steep bluff northward, where we come to the wagon-road from the Mammoth Hot Springs. A ride of three miles from here, through open groves and down frequent grades, brings you to

BARONETT'S BRIDGE, across and near the forks of the Yellowstone. This bridge was built years ago for the accommodation of miners going to Clark's Fork mines (now Cook

City), about thirty miles eastward from this point. Jack Baronett is the man who found and rescued Mr. Evarts, who was lost in the Park for thirty-seven days, in 1870, and came so near perishing. He is an old-timer, a "mighty hunter," and a famous guide through the Park and adjacent mountains.

Less than two miles west from the camp at this bridge, says Colonel P. W. Norris, is a small lake, and along the steep cliffs to the right, and also to the north, are trunks of PETRIFIED TREES still standing, which are from two to fifteen or twenty feet high. They are quite ancient, and many have fallen down. It is a fine place to gather fragments of the fossilized wood, and also specimens of chalcedony, agate, amethyst, and other singular formations. They are well worth a visit from lovers of such curiosities.

From the bridge, a ride of thirteen miles, with several fine camping places on the route, brings you to

EAST GARDINER FALLS, another picturesque little cascade— a succession of falls about forty feet high, near the road to the left, hidden away under the pines as you follow down the stream. It will take but a short time to stop and see them, after which a drive of three or four miles, crossing East Gardiner River on the way, brings the tourist back to the starting-point at Mammoth Springs.

The trip closing here constitutes the Grand Rounds, and includes the objects of general interest to the tourist visiting the Yellowstone Park.

REGION EAST OF THE YELLOWSTONE RIVER

Although we have gone over most of the Park that is generally visited by tourists, yet on the east side of Yellowstone River there is a vast extent of country, broken by high mountains and carved by deep cañons, which, though it abounds with curiosities, yet hardly justifies a visit except from the scientist or gentleman of leisure.

The Clark's Fork Mines are reached by an old and much-used trail leading from Baronett's Bridge eastward up the East Fork of the Yellowstone. They are twenty-seven miles distant, near the eastern limit of the Park, and contain some quartz ledges of considerable promise.

FOSSIL FORESTS abound in the basin of the East Fork, Pelican, Tower, and Black Tail creeks. Some of the finest specimens are found on Amethyst Mountain. On parts of the mountain's face the trunks of great petrified trees stand along the ledges like the columns of an old temple. The mountain abounds with trunks and limbs of trees turned into stone. Beautiful specimens of agate and crystals of every tint are to be found; also in the underlying strata are found remains of toads, snakes, and fishes.

SODA BUTTE HOT SPRINGS are on the Miner's Trail, fifteen miles south-east of the bridge, and are noted for the medicinal properties of their waters, which are strongly impregnated with soda.

HOODOO REGION, OR GOBLIN LAND, is the term that has been applied by miners and trappers to a section of country about forty-five miles south-east of Baronett's Bridge, noted for the countless formations so wild and quaint that they were called "Hoodoos," or "Goblins." "Hoodoo Mountain," says Colonel Norris, "is evidently of volcanic origin, and was eroded into its present form. Upon its southern face it is still changing. Here, extending from five hundred to fifteen hundred feet below the summit, the frosts and storms of untold ages in an Alpine climate have worn about a dozen labyrinths of countless deep, narrow, tortuous channels amid the long, slender, tottering pillars, shafts, and spires of the conglomerate breccia and other remaining volcanic rocks. In shape they are unlike any elsewhere known, being a cross between the usual spire and the steeple form, and the slender-based and flat, tottering, table-topped sandstone monuments near the Garden of the Gods in Colorado; and while lacking the beauty of these, surpass both in wild, weird fascination. The sharp-cornered fragments of rocks of nearly every formation and shade of coloring, by a peculiar volcanic cement attached sidewise, endwise, and upon the tops, sides, and apparently unsupported, upon each other, represent every form, garb, and position of gigantic human beings, as well as of birds, beasts, and reptiles. In fact, nearly every form, animate or inanimate, real or chimerical, ever actually seen or conjured by the imagination, may be here observed."

But it is not advisable to go there at present without a good guide.

ANIMALS IN THE PARK.

Several herds of mountain bison, or buffalo, roam through different portions of the Park. They have been seen upon the mountain spurs and grassy valleys of East Fork of the Yellowstone and Soda Butte, and another herd has been discerned on the Madison Plateau and Little Madison in the western portion of the Park. They are also found in various parks along the Rocky Mountain range. Colonel Norris says that they are "somewhat smaller, of lighter color, less curly, and with horns smaller and less spreading than those of the bison that formerly inhabited the great parks of Colorado."

There are also elk, moose, white-tailed deer, black-tailed deer, prong-horned antelope, big-horned sheep, six varieties of the bear tribe, besides the "wolverine, or long-tailed mud bear." Then, there are the gray, or buffalo wolf, the coyote, and another species of a dark-brown color. There are skunks, foxes of various colors—red, gray, and black—badgers, "rock-dogs" (similar to wood-chuck or ground-hog), porcupines, rabbits (jack, and a small species of cotton-tail, seldom seen), sedge-rat, and mountain-rat, mice, burrowing moles, squirrels (small, of a dark-brown color), chip-munks, beaver, otter, mink, and musk-rats. None of these are so numerous as to be pestiferous. The larger game is kept back in the mountains from the road, and it hardly pays to hunt it.

CLIMATE.

Notwithstanding the great altitude of this region, yet even the winters are not so cold as would be expected. For the

DIRECTIONS FOR TOURISTS. 213

benefit of the reader the following table, compiled from the official reports of P. W. Norris, is given, as showing the condition of the weather at Mammoth Springs for the successive years during the months named:

For July.
1879. Sunrise, 59°; midday, 80°; sunset, 63°; mean, 67°.
1880. Sunrise, 50°; midday, 68°; sunset, 62°; mean, 60°.
1881. Sunrise, 55°; midday, 77°; sunset, 69°; mean, 67°.

For August.
1879. Sunrise, 49°; midday, 74°; sunset, 69°; mean, 64°.
1880. Sunrise, 50°; midday, 68°; sunset, 64°; mean, 61°.
1881. Sunrise, 50°; midday, 79°; sunset, 66°; mean, 65°.

For September.
1879. Sunrise, 39°; midday, 60°; sunset, 53°; mean, 51°.
1880. Sunrise, 41°; midday, 66°; sunset, 58°; mean, 55°.
1881. Sunrise, 36°; midday, 61°; sunset, 50°; mean, 46°.

For October.
1879. Sunrise, 41°; midday, 57°; sunset, 52°; mean, 50°.
1880. Sunrise, 32°; midday, 57°; sunset, 42°; mean, 44°.
1881. Sunrise, 29°; midday, 49°; sunset, 39°; mean, 39°.

DISTANCES OF ROUTES TO THE NATIONAL PARK.

Southern Route.

	Miles.
Omaha to Beaver Cañon, *via* Ogden	1,304
Beaver Cañon to Lower Geyser Basin (Bassett's stage line, two days)	100
Omaha to Lower Geyser Basin, total	1,404
Omaha to Lower Geyser Basin, *via* Oregon Short Line from Granger	1,307

Northern Route.

St. Paul to Livingstone (Northern Pacific Railway)	1,030
Livingstone to Mammoth Hot Springs	57
St. Paul to Mammoth Hot Springs, total	1,087

WAGON-ROADS.

Beaver Cañon Route.

	Between Points.	Total.
Beaver Cañon to Lower Geyser Basin...............		100

Virginia City Route.

Dillon to Virginia City, daily coach......................		65
Butte City to Virginia City (about)...................		80
Virginia City to Henry's Lake........................		60
Henry's Lake to Riverside (good camp and fishing)...	22	82
Lookout Cliffs...	4	86
Marshall's Hotel in Firehole Basin.	8	94
Prospect Point	1	95

Bozeman Route.

Bozeman to Mouth of Cañon.............................		4
Yellowstone Valley, near mouth of Trail Creek..	20	24
Bottler's Ranch on Yellowstone........................	16	40
Cinnabar (terminus of railroad from Livingstone)	28	68
Mammoth Hot Springs................................	6	74

ROUTES WITHIN THE PARK.

Bridle-path.

Mammoth Hot Springs to Middle Gardiner Falls, and return		8

WAGON-ROAD TO GEYSER BASINS.

Mammoth Springs to Terrace Pass		2
Swan Lake Camp...	3	5
Crossing of Middle Fork of Gardiner's River......	2½	7½
Willow Park Camp...	3½	11
Cold Springs...	1	12
Obsidian Cliffs and Beaver Lake......................	1	13
Green Creek (poison water)..............................	1	14
Lake of the Woods...	1	15
Norris Valley (good camps).............................	2	17
Norris Fork Crossing (good camp)..................	3	20
Norris Geyser Basin	1	21

DIRECTIONS FOR TOURISTS. 215

	Between Points.	Total
Geyser Creek (forks of trail leading to Paint Pots)........	3	24
Head of Gibbon Cañon and foot-bridge leading to Monument Geysers........	1	25
Falls of Gibbon........	4	29
Cañon Creek (half mile below camp)........	½	29½
Earthquake Cliffs........	2½	32
Lookout Terrace........	2	34
Marshall's Hotel at Forks of Firehole River......	3	37
Marshall's Hotel to Queen's Laundry and return		6
Prospect Point........	1	38
Camp Reunion........	1	39
Camp Reunion to Midway Geyser Basin........	3	42
Old Faithful (in Upper Geyser Basin)........	6	48
Return to Lower Geyser Basin........	10	58

Bridle-path from Upper Firehole direct to Yellowstone Lake.

Kepler's Cascades........		2
Norris Pass of Rocky Mountains........	6	8
Delacy's Creek and Camp (Pacific waters)........	1	9
Two Ocean Pond (Rocky Mountain summit)......	3½	12½
Thumb of Yellowstone Lake (camp near Hot Springs)........	3	15½
Hot Springs Creek (poor camp)........	6½	22
Natural Bridge........	6	28
Outlet of Yellowstone Lake (camp; trail meets wagon-road)........	5	33

Wagon-road from Lower Firehole Basin to Yellowstone Lake, Sulphur Mountain, Mud Geyser, Great Falls, and Grand Cañon.

Lower Basin to Rocky Fork Camp........		5
Willow Camp........	2	7
Mary's Lake (near divide)........	4	11
Alum Creek Camp........	3	14
Sage Creek (forks of road)........	7	21
Muddy Geyser (near Nez Perce Ford)........	2	23
Outlet of Yellowstone Lake........	6	29

216 YELLOWSTONE PARK.

	Between Points.	Total
Return to Sage Creek (forks of road)	8	37
Sulphur Mountain	1½	38½
Mouth of Alum Creek	1½	40
Upper Falls of Yellowstone	3	43

Bridle-path from Yellowstone Falls and Cañon to Tower Falls.

Summit of Mount Washburne		10
Tower Falls (camp)	7	17

Road from Top of Bluff at Tower Falls to Mammoth Springs.

Forks of Yellowstone, or Baronett's Bridge		3
Pleasant Valley	2	5
Dry Cañon, or Devil's Cut	2	7
Lava Beds	4	11
Black-tail Deer Creek	2	13
Upper Falls of the East Gardiner	3	16
Mammoth Hot Springs	4	20

Miner's Trail to Clark Fork Mines.

Baronett's Bridge to Amethyst Creek		10
Crossing East Fork of Yellowstone River	2	12
Soda Butte (medicinal springs near gamekeeper's cabin)	3	15
Trout Lake	2	17
Round Prairie	3	20
North Line of Wyoming	4	24
Clark's Fork Pass, Creek City, and mines	3	27

Hoodoo or Goblin Mountain Bridle-path.

Gamekeeper's cabin (near Soda Butte) to Hot Sulphur Springs		2
Ford of Cache Creek	1	3
Alum Springs and return	4	7
Calfee Creek	4	11
Miller's Creek	2	13
Mountain Terrace	8	21
Old Camp	5	26

	Between Points.	Total.
Golden Labyrinths	2	28
Monument on Hoodoo or Goblin Mountain	1	29

Fossil Forest Bridle-path.

	Between Points.	Total.
Gamekeeper's cabin to foot of Amethyst Mountain		3
Summit of Amethyst Mountain	3	6
Orange Creek	5	11
Sulphur Hills	4	15
Forks of Pelican Creek	8	23
Indian Pond at Concretion Cove on Yellowstone Lake	5	28
Lower Ford of Pelican Creek	3	31
Foot of Yellowstone Lake	3	34

Nez Perce Bridle-path.

	Between Points.	Total.
Indian Pond to Pelican Valley		3
Ford of Pelican Creek	3	6
Nez Perce Ford of the Yellowstone	6	12

Mount Washburne Bridle-path.

	Between Points.	Total.
Great Falls to Cascade Creek Camp		2
Spur of Mount Washburne (ascend a mile)	8	10
Forks of Bridle-paths	4	14
Tower Falls Camp	3	17

Passamaria or Stinking Water Bridle-path.

	Between Points.	Total.
Concretion Cove to Turbid Lake		3
Jones's Pass of the Sierra Shoshone Range	7	10
Confluence of the Jones and Stinking Water Fork of the Passamaria River	5	15

ALTITUDES OF VARIOUS PLACES, FROM OFFICIAL REPORTS.

	Feet.
Upper Geyser Basin	7,300
Midway Geyser Basin	7,296
Lower Geyser Basin	7,260
Shoshone Geyser Basin	7,880
Hot Springs, Yellowstone Lake	7,788
Mammoth Hot Springs	6,387
Mount Washburne	10,388
Divide between Madison and Yellowstone	8,164
Yellowstone Falls	7,693
Yellowstone Lake	7,738
Mouth of Tower Creek	6,207
Henry's Lake	6,443
Bozeman, Montana	4,900
Virginia City, Montana	5,824
Butte, Montana	5,800
Helena, Montana	4,266
Deer Lodge	4,546
Fort Benton	2,780
Gallatin City	4,838
Missoula	3,900
Whitehall	4,639
Bannack	5,896
Bridger's Pass	9,147
Mullen's Pass	5,980
Pleasant Valley Pass	6,030
Emigrant Peak	10,629
Mount Powell	10,500

www.ingramcontent.com/pod-product-compliance
Lightning Source LLC
Chambersburg PA
CBHW031729230426
43669CB00007B/300